United States
Department
of Agriculture

Forest Service

**Rocky Mountain
Research Station**

Resource Bulletin
RMRS-RB-11

December 2010

Colorado's Forest Resources, 2002-2006

**Michael T. Thompson, Joseph A. Duda,
Larry T. DeBlander, John D. Shaw, Chris Witt,
Todd A. Morgan, and Michael C. Amacher**

This report presents a summary of the most recent inventory information for Colorado's forest lands. The report includes descriptive highlights and tables of area, number of trees, biomass, volume, growth, mortality, and removals. Most of the tables are organized by forest type, species, diameter class, or owner group. The report also describes inventory design, inventory terminology, and data reliability. Results show that Colorado's forest land totals 23 million acres. Nearly 50 percent of this forest land is administered by the USDA Forest Service. Pinyon-juniper forests cover over 5.5 million acres whereas forest comprised of fir, spruce, and hemlock comprise 24 percent of Colorado's forest land. Aspen is the single most abundant tree species in Colorado. Net annual growth of all live trees 5.0 inches diameter and greater on Colorado forest land totaled 219.6 million cubic feet. Average annual mortality totaled nearly 421.0 million cubic feet.

The Authors

Michael T. Thompson is a Forester and a member of the Analysis Team with the Interior West Inventory and Analysis Program at the USFS Rocky Mountain Research Station in Ogden, Utah. He holds a B.S. degree in forestry from North Carolina State University (contact: mtthompson@fs.fed.us, 801-625-5374).

Joseph A. Duda is the Forest Management Division Supervisor of the Colorado State Forest Service. He holds a B.S. degree in forestry from Michigan Technical University.

Larry T. DeBlander is a Forester and a member of the Analysis Team with the Interior West Inventory and Analysis Program at the USFS Rocky Mountain Research Station in Ogden, Utah. He holds a B.S. degree in Forest Science from Pennsylvania State University.

John D. Shaw is a Forester and Analysis Team Leader with the Interior West Inventory and Analysis Program at the USFS Rocky Mountain Research Station in Ogden, Utah. He holds B.S. and M.S. degrees in Natural Resources Management from the University of Alaska, Fairbanks and a Ph.D. in Forest Ecology from Utah State University.

Chris Witt is an Ecologist and a member of the Analysis Team with the Interior West Inventory and Analysis Program at the USFS Rocky Mountain Research Station in Ogden, UT. He holds B.S. and M.S. degrees in Ecology from Idaho State University.

Todd A. Morgan is the director of the Forest Industry Research Program at The University of Montana's Bureau of Business and Economic Research in Missoula, Montana. He received a B.A. degree in Philosophy and a B.S. degree in Forest Science from Pennsylvania State University and an M.S. degree in Forestry from The University of Montana.

Michael C. Amacher is a Research Soil Scientist in the Forest and Woodland Ecosystems Research Program at the USFS Rocky Mountain Research Station in Logan, Utah. He also serves as the western soils Indicator Advisor in the Indicators of Forest Health program. He has B.S. and M.S. degrees in chemistry and a Ph.D. in soil chemistry, all from The Pennsylvania State University.

Acknowledgments _____

The Rocky Mountain Research Station gratefully acknowledges the Colorado State Forest Service for its role in collecting the field data. The Rocky Mountain Research Station also gratefully acknowledges the cooperation and assistance of the Rocky Mountain Region, Forest Service, U.S. Department of Agriculture; the Bureaus of Land Management and Indian Affairs; and the National Park Service, U.S. Department of the Interior. The authors extend a special note of thanks to private landowners who provided information and access to field sample plots.

Report Highlights _____

Forest Area

- Colorado's forest land area totals 23 million acres.

- Unreserved forest land accounts for most (88 percent) of the forest land in Colorado and totals 20 million acres.

- Fifty-seven percent of Colorado's unreserved forest land is classified as timberland and 43 percent is classified as unproductive forest land.

- Nearly 50 percent of Colorado's total forest land area, about 11.1 million acres, is administered by the USDA Forest Service.

- Pinyon-juniper forests cover over 5.5 million acres and account for 24 percent of forest land in Colorado.

- The fir-spruce-mountain hemlock forest type group totals nearly 4.7 million acres.

- Aspen forest types cover 3.1 million acres and are the third most abundant forest type group.

Numbers of Trees, Volume, and Biomass

- There are an estimated 12.7 billion live trees in Colorado.

- Softwood species total 6.3 billion trees or 49 percent of all live trees.

- Numbers of aspen trees total nearly 1.7 billion, making this species the single most abundant tree in Colorado.

- The net volume of live trees in Colorado on forest land totals 37.3 billion cubic feet.

- Growing-stock volume on timberland in Colorado totals 25 billion cubic feet, or 67 percent of the total live volume on forest land.

- The total weight of oven-dry biomass on Colorado forest land is 676 million tons.

- Net volume of sawtimber trees on timberland totals 92 billion board feet.

Forest Growth and Mortality

- Net annual growth of all live trees 5.0 inches diameter and greater on Colorado forest land totaled 219.6 million cubic feet.

- Average annual mortality totaled nearly 421.0 million cubic feet

- Mortality exceeded net growth for all major tree species except for aspen and western woodland softwoods.

Issues in Colorado's Forest Resources

- Colorado is experiencing one of the largest outbreaks of mountain pine beetle in lodgepole pine forests since records became available for the State.

- As of 2006, the average annual biomass of insect-killed lodgepole pines is 926 thousand dry tons, which represents a nearly threefold increase over the 331 thousand dry tons recorded in 2002.

- Varied observers began noticing rapid mortality of aspen in multiple locations in southwestern Colorado beginning in 2004.

- Unlike bark-beetle caused mortality in lodgepole and ponderosa pine forests, trends in aspen mortality over the annual inventory period in Colorado do not indicate a significant upward trend since 2002.

- It does not appear that the recently observed aspen mortality event is reflected in Colorado's annual inventory, which could be due to (1) the event is relatively recent, (2) the event may be a localized event that impacts aspen in domains too small to be adequately assessed in a broad-scale inventory, (3) diverse factors associated with the decline make causal agents difficult to identify, and (4) aspen stand dynamics are complex.

Forest Health

- The high level of conifer mortality occurring in Colorado is currently of paramount concern.

- Examination of current mortality rates puts a perspective on what the impact might have on the inventory of live trees.

- Conifer mortality rates on National Forest lands, where 78 percent of the conifer mortality is occurring, average over 1.3 percent annually.

- True firs recorded the highest annual conifer mortality rate of 2.5 percent, followed by lodgepole pine at 1.4 percent.

- The high numbers of sapling-size conifers in relation to larger-size conifers indicates sustainable regeneration for the foreseeable future at the State level.

Contents

Colorado's Forest Resources, 2002-2006

Michael T. Thompson
Joseph A. Duda
Larry T. DeBlander
John D. Shaw
Chris Witt
Todd A. Morgan
Michael C. Amacher

Introduction

Colorado's Forest Inventory

This resource bulletin highlights results of Colorado's forest resources as interpreted from the first series of annual forest measurements in the State. Annual surveys of U.S. forests were mandated by the Agricultural Research Extension and Education Reform Act of 1998 (Farm Bill, http://thomas.loc.gov/cgi-bin/query/z?c105:s.1150.enr:). They feature (1) a nationally consistent, fixed-radius, four-point plot configuration; (2) a systematic national sampling design consisting of a national base grid where each plot represents approximately 6,000 acres; (3) integration of the forest inventory and forest health monitoring sampling designs; (4) annual measurement of a fixed proportion of permanent plots; (5) reporting of data or data summaries within 6 months after yearly sampling; (6) a default 5- to 10-year moving average estimator; and (7) a summary report every 5 years.

The Interior West Forest Inventory and Analysis (IWFIA) program and the Colorado State Forest Service (CSFS) began the forest inventory of Colorado's forest resources in 2002. CSFS field crews were responsible for collecting field data and IWFIA personnel were responsible for training CSFS field crews and assuring that measurement procedures were meeting national standards. This joint effort launched the new annual inventory system in which one-tenth of the field plots (considered one panel) are measured each year. In 2006, IWFIA completed measurement of the fifth panel of inventory plots in Colorado. This resource bulletin consolidates data from all five panels in the first cycle of annual measurements and uses that information to describe the current issues affecting the status and condition of the State's forests. Past inventories of Colorado were referred to as periodic inventories where estimates were derived from measurements of all plots in the State over a period of 2 to 3 years. Two previous inventories of Colorado's forest resources were completed in 1983 and 1959 (Benson and Green 1987; Miller and Choate 1964).

Comparison with Previous Inventories

Data from new inventories are often compared with data from earlier inventories to determine trends in forest resources. However, for the comparisons to be valid, the procedures used in the two inventories must be compatible. There are three significant factors that cause incompatibility between the 2006 annual inventory of Colorado and the previous periodic inventory completed in 1983 (Benson and Green 1987).

USDA Forest Service Resour. Bull. RMRS-RB-11. 2010

1

Inventory procedures—The first factor is that inventory procedures varied by major ownership category in the previous inventory. In 1983, lands controlled by National Forest Systems (NFS) and Bureau of Land Management (BLM) were not inventoried by IWFIA. The forest inventory estimates such as forest area, volume, growth, and mortality were supplied to IWFIA by NFS and BLM. IWFIA only measured inventory plots on lands owned by State agencies and private individuals. The 1983 report merged this inventory data from the different sources to describe the status and condition of Colorado's forest resources. In the 2006 annual inventory, forest resource data were collected by IWFIA and CSFS on all lands meeting the definition of forest land regardless of the species of trees present, ownership status, or administrative status of the land. This includes wilderness areas and other areas in reserved status. The 2006 inventory adhered to all national protocols such as plot configuration, field variables with nationally consistent meanings and measurements, and national precision standards. None of these national protocols were in place in 1983.

Definitions—The second factor is that many definitions of forest resource attributes have changed since 1983. The impact of these changes varies by inventory estimate. Forest land definitions, plot configuration, and procedures used to estimate forest type and stand size are some of the significant changes that have occurred since the previous inventory.

Sampling intensity—The third factor is differences in sampling intensity. The 2006 inventory contains five annual panels of data that represent approximately 50 percent of all inventory plots initially established in Colorado. Therefore, the reduced sample size in the moving average estimation process will result in a higher level of statistical uncertainty compared to a periodic inventory where all plots in the State were measured. This is an important consideration not only when comparing data from previous inventories but also when evaluating forest estimates for small domains. Examples of small domains are individual counties, small groups of counties, individual National Forests, or small ecological provinces.

The 2006 inventory of Colorado's forests marks an important shift from its predecessors, both in the scope of its measurements and in its timeliness. With the resources to measure one 10-percent panel of the total sample locations each year, it is now possible and practical to monitor emerging resource issues by providing yearly "snapshot" updates and longer term trend analysis. The resulting improvements in timeliness, combined with the national effort to standardize national inventory procedures, have transformed Colorado's forest inventory into a tool that can detect short-term trends, address relevant issues, examine ecological relationships, and evaluate human activities that will shape the forests of Colorado for the future.

Timber Products Output

Timber harvest estimates and the composition and operation of the primary forest products industry in Colorado are presented in this report. The major source of data for these studies was a census of primary forest products facilities in Colorado and adjacent States that received timber from Colorado during calendar year 2002. This information is the direct result of a cooperative effort between The University of Montana's Bureau of Business and Economic Research (BBER) and the USDA Forest Service IWFIA program. Together, BBER and Forest Service research stations have been conducting periodic mill censuses in the Rocky Mountains for over 25 years. The Forest Industries Data Collection System (FIDACS) was developed by BBER and IWFIA to collect, compile, and make available State- and county-level information on the operations of the forest products industry and the timber it uses. The FIDACS uses a written questionnaire or phone interview of forest products manufacturers to collect the following information for each facility for a given calendar year: production capacity and employment; volume of raw material received by county and ownership; species of timber received; finished product volumes, types, sales, values, and market locations; and utilization and marketing of manufacturing residue. Information collected through the FIDACS is processed, analyzed, and stored at the BBER in Missoula, Montana. Additional information is available by request; however, individual firm-level data are confidential and will not be released.

Inventory Methods

Plot Configuration

The national FIA plot design consists of four 24-foot radius subplots configured as a central subplot and three peripheral subplots. Centers of the peripheral subplots are located at distances of 120 feet and at azimuths of 0 degrees, 120 degrees, and 240 degrees from the center of the central subplot. Each standing tree with a diameter at breast height (d.b.h.) or diameter at root collar (d.r.c.) 5-inches or larger is measured on these subplots. Each subplot contains a 6.8-foot radius microplot with the center located 12 feet east of the subplot center on which each tree with a d.b.h./d.r.c. from 1.0-inch to 4.9-inches is measured.

In addition to the trees measured on FIA plots, data are also gathered about the area or setting in which the trees are located. Area classifications are useful for partitioning the forest into meaningful categories for analysis. Some of these area attributes are measured (e.g., percent slope), some are assigned by definition (e.g., ownership group), and some are computed from tree data (e.g., percent stocking).

To enable division of the forest into various domains of interest for analysis, it is important that the tree data recorded on these plots are properly associated with the area classifications. To accomplish this, plots are mapped by condition class. Field crews assign an arbitrary number to the first condition class encountered on a plot. This number is then defined by a series of predetermined discrete variables attached to it (i.e., land use, stand size, regeneration status, tree density, stand origin, ownership group, and disturbance history). Additional conditions are identified if there is a distinct change in any of the condition-class variables on the plot.

Sample Design

Based on historic national standards, a sampling intensity of approximately one plot per 6,000 acres is necessary to satisfy national FIA precision guidelines. Therefore, FIA divided the area of the United States into nonoverlapping, 5,937-acre hexagons and established a plot in each hexagon using procedures designed to preserve existing plot locations from previous inventories. This base sample, designated as the Federal base sample, was systematically divided into a number of interpenetrating, nonoverlapping panels, each of which provides complete, systematic coverage of the State. Each year the plots in a single panel are measured, and panels are selected on either a 5-year (eastern regions) or 10-year (western regions) rotating basis (Reams and Van Deusen 1999). For estimation purposes, the measurement of each panel of plots is considered an independent, equal probability sample of all lands in a State.

USDA Forest Service Resour. Bull. RMRS-RB-11. 2010

3

Three-Phase Inventory

FIA conducts inventories in three phases, which are discussed in detail below. Phase 1 uses remotely sensed data to obtain initial plot land cover observations and to stratify land area in the population of interest to increase the precision of estimates. In Phase 2, field crews visit the physical locations of permanent field plots to measure traditional inventory variables such as tree species, diameter, and height. In Phase 3, field crews visit a subset of Phase 2 plots to obtain measurements for an additional suite of variables associated with forest and ecosystem health.

Phase 1—Remotely sensed data in the form of aerial photographs, digital orthoquads, and satellite imagery are used for initial plot establishment. Spatial analysts determine a digitized geographic location for each field plot, and a human interpreter determines whether a plot location has the potential to sample forest land. Plot locations with the potential to sample forest land and that are accessible to field crews are selected for further measurement by field crew visits in Phase 2.

The remote sensing medium used for stratification in Colorado was 2004 MODIS satellite imagery. The spatial resolution of the MODIS imagery used was 250 meters. Three strata were recognized: forest land, nonforest land, and census water. The spatial resolution of the imagery was 250 meters. Depending on geography and sampling intensity, areas are identified within a State for area computation and are referred to as estimation units. In Colorado, individual counties served as the estimation units. Each estimation unit's area is divided into strata of known size using the satellite imagery and computer-aided classification. The classified imagery divides the total area of the estimation unit into pixels of equal size and assigns each pixel to one of H strata. Each stratum, h, then contains n_h ground plots where the Phase 2 attributes of interest are observed.

To illustrate, the area estimator for forest land for an estimation unit in Colorado is defined as:

$$\hat{A}_g = A_{Tg} \sum_{h=1}^{H} \frac{n'_{hg}}{n'_g} \frac{\displaystyle\sum_{i=1}^{n_{hg}} y_{ihg}}{n_{hg}}$$

where:

$\hat{A}_g$ = total forest area (acres) for estimation unit g

A_{Tg} = total land area (acres) in estimation unit g

H = number of strata

n'_{hg} = number of Phase 1 points in stratum h in estimation unit g

n'_g = total number of Phase 1 points in estimation unit g

y_{ihg} = forest land condition proportion on Phase 2 plot i in stratum h in estimation unit g

n_{hg} = number of Phase 2 plots in stratum h in estimation unit g

Phase 2—Field crews record a variety of data for plot locations determined in Phase 1 to sample accessible forest land. Before visiting plot locations, field crews consult county land records to determine the ownership of plots and then seek permission from private landowners to measure plots on their lands. The field crews determine the location of the geographic center of the center subplot using geographic positioning system (GPS) receivers. They record condition-level observations that include land use, forest type, stand origin, stand-size class, site productivity class, forest disturbance history, slope, aspect, and physiographic class. For each tree, field crews record a variety of observations and measurements including species, live/dead status, lean, diameter, height, crown ratio, crown class, damage, and decay status. Office staff use statistical models based on field crew measurements to calculate values for additional variables including individual tree volume and per unit area estimates of number of trees, volume, biomass, growth, and mortality.

Phase 3—The third phase of the enhanced FIA program focuses on forest health. Phase 3 is administered cooperatively by the FIA program, other Forest Service programs, other Federal agencies, State natural resource agencies, and universities, and it is partially integrated with the Forest Health Monitoring (FHM) program. The ground survey portion of the FHM program was integrated into the FIA program as Phase 3 in 1999. The Phase 3 sample consists of a 1:16 subset of the Phase 2 plots with one Phase 3 plot for approximately every 95,000 acres. Phase 3 measurements are obtained by field crews during the growing season and include an extended suite of ecological data. Because each Phase 3 plot is also a Phase 2 plot, the entire suite of Phase 2 measurements is collected on each Phase 3 plot at the same time as the Phase 3 measurements.

Sources of Error

Sampling error—The process of sampling (selecting a random subset of a population and calculating estimates from this subset) causes estimates to contain error they would not have if every member of the population had been observed and included in the estimate. The 2002-2006 FIA inventory of Colorado is based on a sample of 5,595 plots systematically located across the State (a total area of 66.6 million acres), a sampling rate of approximately one plot for every 11,900 acres.

The statistical estimation procedures are described in detail in Bechtold and Patterson (2005) and provide the estimates of the population totals and means presented in this report. Along with every estimate is an associated sampling error that is typically expressed as a percentage of the estimated value but that can also be expressed in the same units as the estimate or as a confidence interval (the estimated value plus or minus the sampling error). This sampling error is the primary measure of the reliability of an estimate. A sampling error can be interpreted to mean that the chances are two out of three that had 100-percent inventory been taken using these methods, the results would have been within the limits indicated. The sampling errors for State-level estimates are presented in Appendix D, table 37.

Users may compute statistical confidence for subdivisions of the reported data using the formula below. Because sampling error increases as the area or volume considered decreases, users should aggregate data categories as much as possible. Sampling errors obtained from this method are only approximations of reliability because homogeneity of variances is assumed. The formula is:

$$SE_s = SE_t \frac{\sqrt{X_t}}{\sqrt{X_s}}$$

SE_s = sampling error for subdivision of State total.

SE_t = sampling error for State total.

X_s = sum of values for the variable of interest (area, volume, biomass, etc.) for subdivision of State total.

X_t = sum of values (area, volume, biomass, etc.) for State total.

Measurement error—Errors associated with the methods and instruments used to observe and record the sample attributes are called measurement errors. On FIA plots, attributes such as the diameter and height of a tree are measured with different instruments, and other attributes such as species and crown class are observed without the aid of an instrument. On a typical FIA plot, 30 to 70 trees are observed with 15 to 20 attributes recorded on each tree. In addition, many attributes that describe the plot and conditions on the plot are observed. Errors in any of these observations affect the quality of the estimates. If a measurement is biased (such as tree diameter consistently taken at an incorrect place on the tree), then the estimates that use this observation (such as calculated volume) will reflect this bias. Even if measurements are unbiased, high levels of random error in the measurements will add to the total random error of the estimation process.

To ensure that all FIA observations are made to the highest standards possible, a regular program of quality control and quality assurance is an integral part of all FIA data collection efforts. This program begins with the documentation of protocols and procedures used in the inventory followed by extensive crew training. To assess the quality of the data collected by these trained crews, a random sample of plots are measured independently by a different qualified crew—referred to as blind checks. The measurement on these blind check plots is done by a crew termed the QA crews. In all cases, QA crews have as much or more experience and training in FIA field measurements as the standard FIA crews.

The quality of field measurements is assessed nationally through a set of measurement quality objectives (MQO's) that are set for every data item FIA collects. Each MQO consists of two parts: a tolerance or acceptable level of measurement error, and an objective interval of the percent of measurements within tolerance. The blind check measurements are used to observe how often individual field crews are meeting these objectives and to assess the overall compliance among all crews. QA results for the Colorado inventory are illustrated in tables E6 and E7.

Prediction error—Errors associated with using mathematical models (such as volume models) to provide observations of the attributes of interest based on sample attributes are referred to as prediction errors. Area, number of trees, volume, biomass, growth, removals, and mortality are the primary attributes of interest presented in this report. Area and number of trees estimates are based on direct observation and do not involve the use of prediction models; however, FIA estimates of volume, biomass, growth, and mortality used model-based predictions in the estimation process. Models are used to predict volume and biomass estimates of individual tree volumes.

Overview of Tables

Forest Inventory and Analysis is currently working on a revised National Core Table set that will expand the suite of tabled information to incorporate more of the core FIA Program, using both Phase 2 and 3 data. Appendix D contains an interim set of tables supporting this report, using Colorado annual data for the years 2002 through 2006. There are a total of 37 tables with statistics for land area, number of trees, wood volume, biomass (weight), growth, mortality, and sampling errors. Table 1 is the only table that includes all land types or land status; the rest include only accessible forest land or timberland. Table 37 shows sampling errors for area, volume, net growth, and mortality at the 67 percent confidence level. Inventory cycle (cycle 2) is a number assigned to a set of plots measured over a particular period of time from which a state estimate using all possible plots is obtained. Additional tables that supplement specific sections are in Appendix E and are numbered consecutively as they appear, starting with table E1.

Overview of Colorado's Forest Resources_____

Ecoregion Provinces of Colorado

Issues and events that influence forest conditions often occur across forest types, ownerships, and political boundaries. As a result, scientists, researchers, and land managers must also find a way to assess and treat these issues in a boundary-less way. Ecoregions are often used as a non-political land division to help researchers study forest conditions. An ecoregion is a large landscape area that has relatively consistent patterns of topography, geology, soils, vegetation, climate, and natural processes (Shinneman and others 2000). Many smaller ecosystems may reside within an ecoregion.

Colorado is at the confluence of seven ecoprovinces (Bailey 1995): (1) the Colorado Plateau Semi-Desert Province in the southwestern part of the State, (2) the Great Plains-Palouse Dry Steppe Province encompasses most of the eastern part of the State, (3) the Intermountain Semi-Desert Province in the northern part, (4) the Intermountain Semi-Desert and Desert Province in the west, (5) the Nevada-Utah Mountains-Semi-Desert Province in the northwest, (6) the Southern Rocky Mountain Steppe Province in the central and western part of the State, and (7) the Arizona-New Mexico Mountains Semi-Desert that occupies a very small portion in the southern region of Colorado.

The most prominent ecoprovince is the Southern Rocky Mountain Steppe, which contains the most forested area and greatest variety of forest types. This region is home to the Rocky Mountains, rugged glaciated mountains as high as 14,000 feet. Forests in this province are characterized by vegetational zonation, controlled by a combination of altitude, latitude, direction of prevailing winds, and slope exposure. The uppermost vegetational zone is characterized by alpine tundra and the absence of trees. Directly below it is the subalpine zone, dominated in most places by Engelmann spruce and subalpine fir. Below this area lies the montane zone, characterized by ponderosa pine and Douglas-fir. Fire disturbance regimes create stands of aspen or lodgepole pine in the subalpine and montane zones. Below the montane belt is the foothill zone. Dry rocky slopes abound in this province, and ponderosa pine and pinyon-juniper are the typical forest types found, depending on slope exposure.

The Great Plains-Palouse Dry Steppe Province is characterized by rolling plains and tablelands of moderate relief in a broad belt that slopes gradually eastward from an altitude of 5,500 ft (1,520 m) near the foot of the Rocky Mountains. This region, often referred to as the Great Plains grasslands, has scattered trees, shrubs, and supports many species of grass. Forests are nearly nonexistent in this province.

The remaining four ecoregion provinces are characterized by dry rocky foothills, mesas, and plateaus. The predominate forest types in these regions are pinyon pine, juniper, or a mix of both commonly referred to as pinyon-juniper woodlands. The forests in these semi-desert regions are commonly associated with sagebrush communities.

Forest Land Classification

Historically, FIA has used a nationally consistent standard for defining different categories of forest land. These categories were originally developed for the purpose of separating forest land deemed suitable for timber production from forest land that was either not suitable or unavailable for timber harvesting activity. The first division of forest land is unreserved forest land and reserved forest land. Unreserved forest land is considered available for harvesting activity where wood volume can be removed for timber products. Reserved forest land is considered unavailable for any type of wood utilization management practice through administrative legislation.

Unreserved forest land is further divided into timberland and unproductive forests. Timberland is forest land capable of producing 20 cubic feet of wood per acre per year of trees designated as a timber species and not withdrawn from timber production. Unproductive forests are, because of species characteristics and site conditions, not capable of producing 20 cubic feet of wood per acre per year of trees designated as a timber species and not withdrawn from timber production (see Standard Forest Inventory and Analysis Terminology).

Reserved forest land is further divided into productive and unproductive forests. Productive forest land is capable of producing 20 cubic feet of wood per acre per year of trees designated as a timber species but is withdrawn from timber production. Unproductive reserved land is, because of a combination of species characteristics and site conditions, not capable of producing 20 cubic feet of wood per acre per year of trees designated as a timber species and withdrawn from timber production (see the "Standard Forest Inventory and Analysis Terminology" section).

The State of Colorado encompasses nearly 67 million acres of land area, of which 23 million acres were estimated by FIA as forest land. Forest land, which FIA generally defines as land with 10 percent or more live tree cover (see Standard Forest Inventory and Analysis Terminology), is primarily located in the central and western regions of Colorado (fig. 1). Unreserved forest land accounts for most (88 percent) of the forest land in Colorado and totals 20 million acres (table 2). Fifty-seven percent of

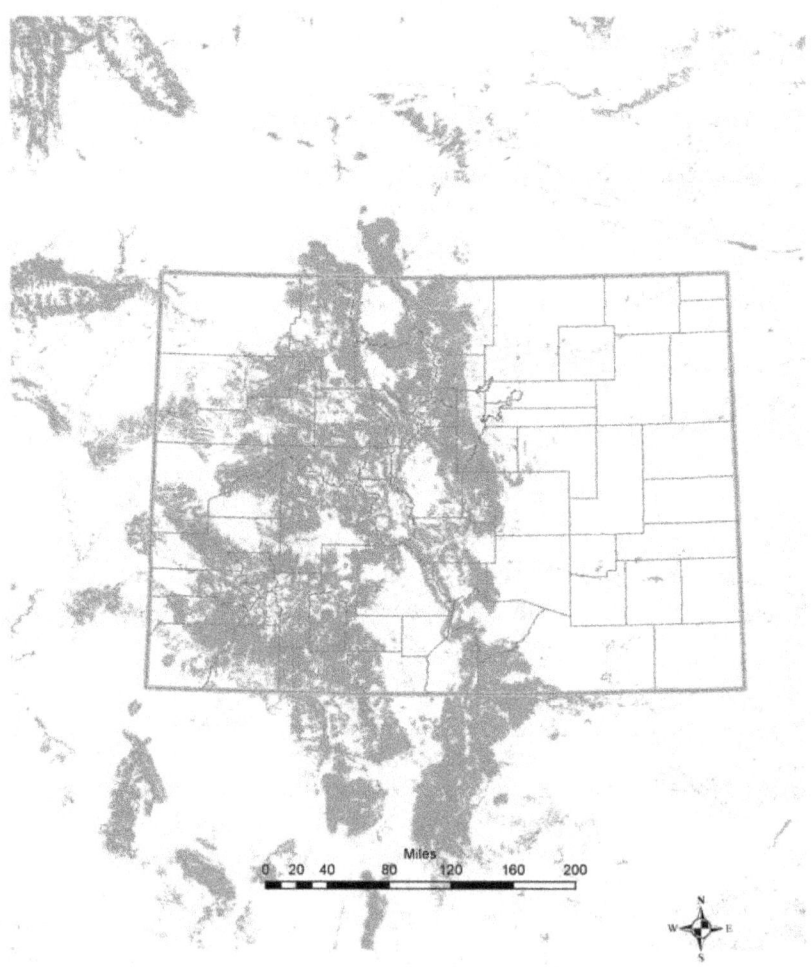

Figure 1—MODIS imagery depicting lands with 10 percent or more tree cover in Colorado, 2002-2006.

8

USDA Forest Service Resour. Bull. RMRS-RB-11. 2010

Colorado's unreserved forest land is classified as timberland and 43 percent is classified as unproductive forest land. Reserved forests account for only 12 percent, or 2.6 million acres, of total forest land and most of this area is classified as productive reserved.

Forest Land Ownership

Nearly 50 percent of Colorado's total forest land area, about 11.1 million acres, is administered by the USDA Forest Service (fig. 2). The National Forest Service System's land in Colorado consists of 10 different National Forests and two National Grasslands. Nearly all of National Forest System's forest land is on land controlled by National Forests with a very small amount occurring on land controlled by National Grasslands. Almost 82 percent of National Forest System's forest land is classified as unreserved forest land. About 7.8 million acres, or 71 percent, of National Forest System's forest land is classified as timberland (table 2).

The other major agency that controls a significant amount of forest land in Colorado is the Bureau of Land Management (BLM). Forest land administered by the BLM totals 4.8 million acres. Most of BLM's forest land—about 95 percent—is classified as unreserved. Only 15 percent of BLM's forest land meets the conditions to qualify as timberland.

Privately owned forest land totals 5.4 million acres. Private landowners are a diverse group in Colorado consisting of private individuals and corporations. All private forest land is in the unreserved owner class and this area is evenly split between the timberland and unproductive category (table 2).

The remaining amount of forest land in Colorado is controlled by the National Park Service (NPS), State and local government, and the Department of Defense. Over 723 thousand acres are controlled by State and local governments, another 339 thousand acres are controlled by the NPS, and 112 thousand acres are controlled by the Department of Defense.

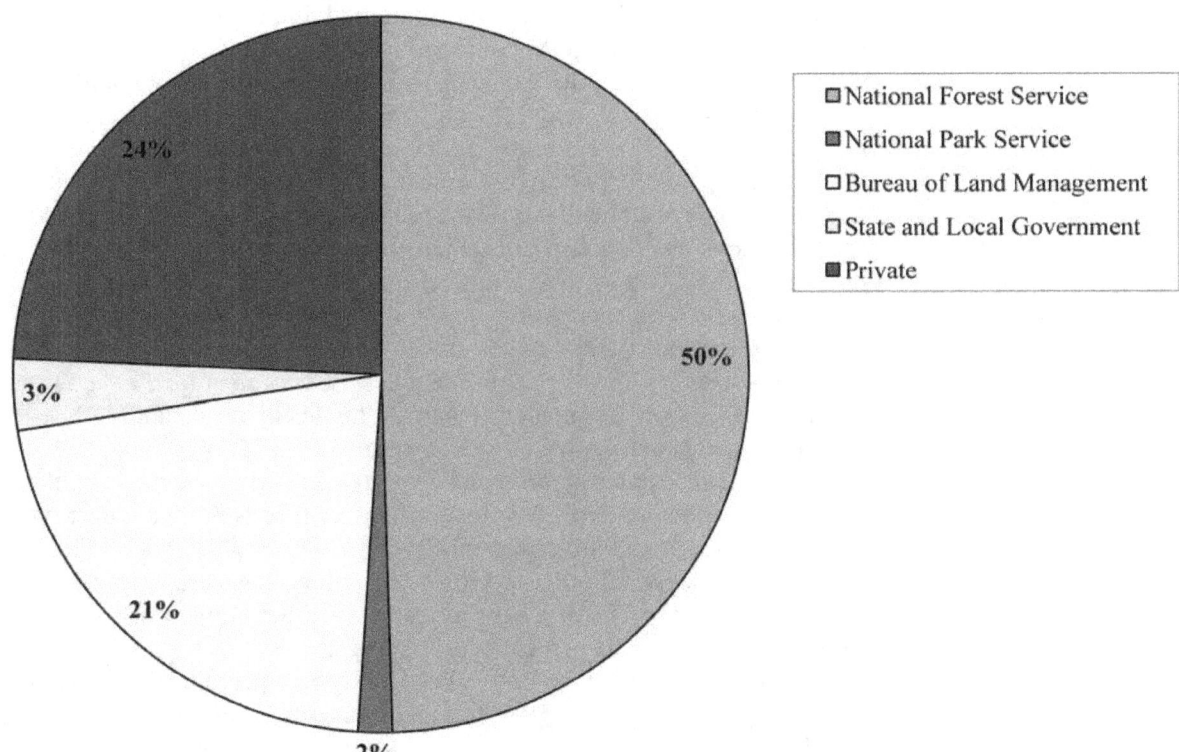

Figure 2— Area of forest land by owner group, Colorado, 2002-2006.

Forest Type

Forest type is a classification of forest land based on the species forming a plurality of living trees growing in a particular forest. The distribution of forest types across the landscape is determined by factors such as climate, soil, elevation, aspect, and disturbance history. Forest type names may be based on a single species or groups of species. Forest types are an important measure of diversity, structure, and successional stage. Loss or gain of a particular forest type over time can be used to assess the impact of major disturbances such as fire, weather, insects, disease, and man-caused disturbances such as timber harvesting activity.

The most abundant forest type group in Colorado is the pinyon-juniper group (fig. 3). Pinyon-juniper forests cover over 5.5 million acres and account for 24 percent of forest land in the State (table 3). Second in abundance, the fir-spruce-mountain hemlock forest type group totals nearly 4.7 million acres. This type group is comprised of subalpine fir, white fir, Engelmann spruce, and Colorado blue spruce. Engelmann spruce accounts for the majority (over 62 percent) of the forest area classified in the fir-spruce-mountain hemlock type group. Aspen forest types cover 3.1 million acres and are the third most abundant forest type group. The gambel oak forest type totals another 2.6 million acres. Lodgepole pine forest types comprise 2.1 million acres or 9 percent of forest area in Colorado. Ponderosa pine and Douglas-fir each account for 1.7 million acres

Stand Age

The present age structure of Colorado's forest area, in terms of stand age and forest type group composition, provides insight into prospective shifts in stand composition over time. On every FIA plot that samples forest land, a stand age is calculated. If there are trees available for suitable increment core extraction, a stand age is estimated based upon the average age of only those trees that fall within the calculated stand-size assignment. For example, suppose an FIA plot sampled a softwood forest type where about 30 percent of the live trees were in the large diameter stand-size (trees at least 9.0 inches d.b.h. and larger) and 70 percent were in the medium diameter stand-size class (trees between 5.0 and 9.0 inches d.b.h.). Since the stand would be classified as a medium diameter stand size class, only the medium size trees would be used in determining stand age. There are limitations to collecting data for stand age computation. Certain tree species, especially those that are very old, prohibit repeatable measures of increment cores. Certain stand types, such as gambel oak, that are predominated with small-diameter trees are very difficult to accurately assign a stand age to. All nonstocked forest conditions—those forested areas that have less than 10 percent stocking of live trees because of disturbance—are assigned a stand age of unclassified.

Most of the forest land in Colorado is between 60 and 120 years of age (table 6). Over 43 percent, or almost 10 million acres, of the forest land is between 60 and 120 years of age. About 12 percent of the forest land is in stands under 21 years of age and less than 6 percent are over 200 years of age.

There is considerable difference in stand age distribution between the major forest type groups in the State (fig. 4). Pinyon-juniper forests are the oldest type group with over half of the forest area in stands over 140 years old. Sixteen percent of pinyon-juniper stands are over 200 years old. Aspen, which is generally shorter lived than most Colorado conifer species, is characterized by a larger number of stands in the younger age classes with over 72 percent of aspen forests in stands 61 to 120 years old and over 10 percent in stands less than 21 years old. Sixty-five percent of the fir-spruce-mountain hemlock type group area is concentrated in stands between 80 and 160 years of age. Of all the major softwood forest types in Colorado, lodgepole pine displays the most even-aged distribution. About 69 percent of lodgepole pine stands are between 60 and 120 years old.

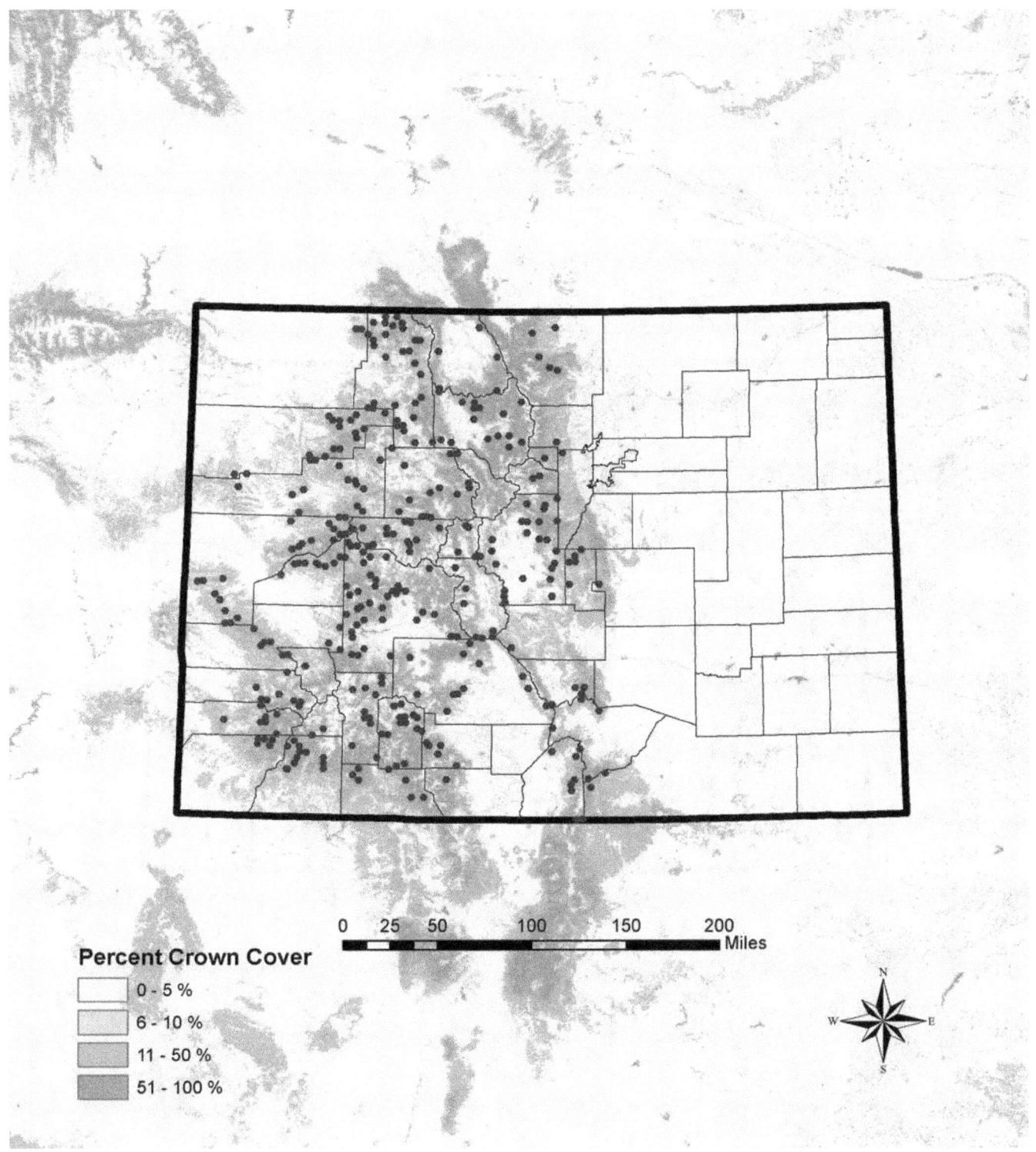

Percent Crown Cover

	0 - 5 %
	6 - 10 %
	11 - 50 %
	51 - 100 %

Aspen 3.1 million acres

Figure 3—FIA plot locations depicting four major forest types in Colorado overlayed on MODIS imagery depicting lands with 4 classes of tree cover in Colorado, 2002-2006. Plot locations have been altered using a procedure defined as fuzzing and swapping.

(continued)

USDA Forest Service Resour. Bull. RMRS-RB-11. 2010

11

Figure 3—(Continued).

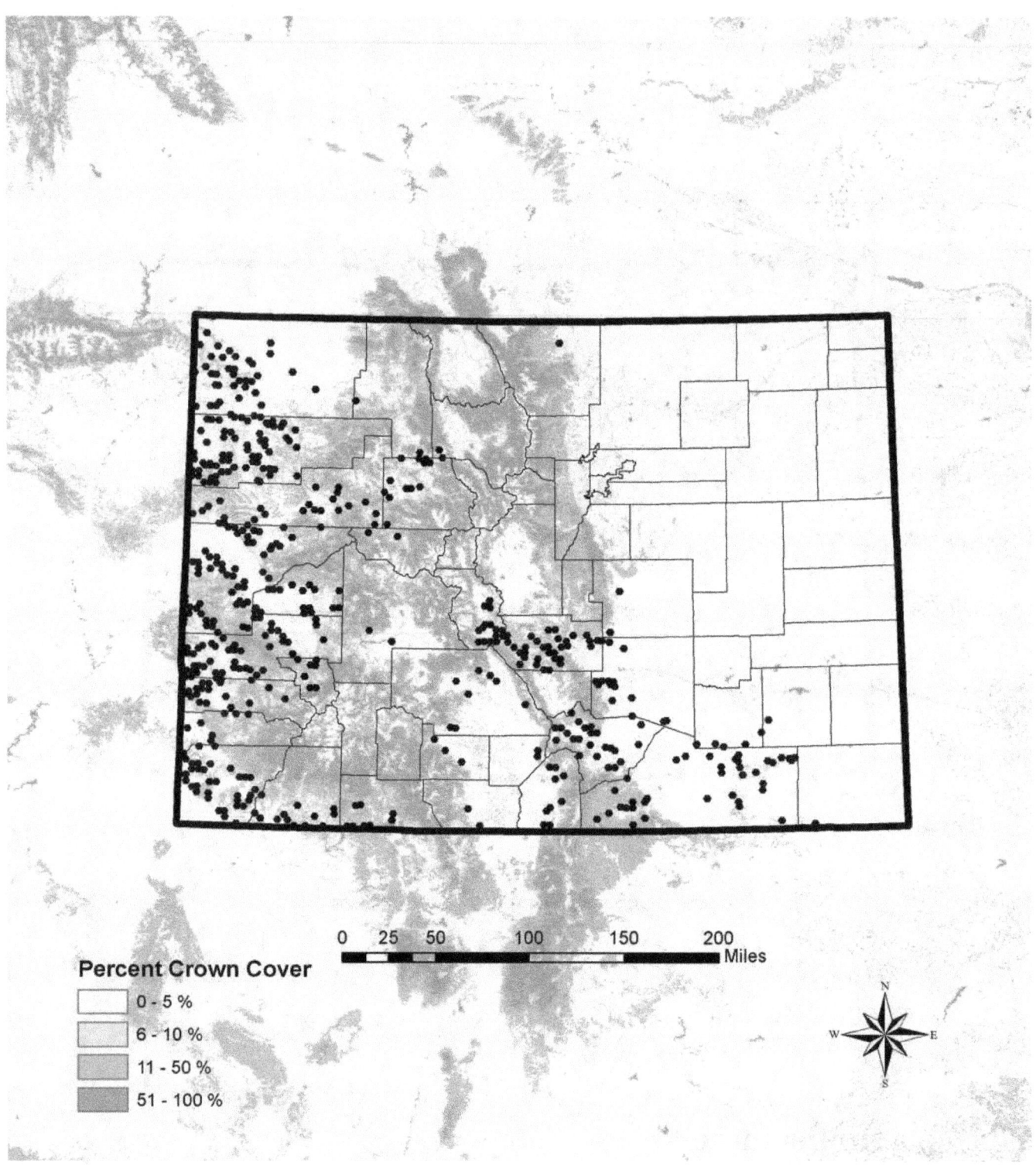

Percent Crown Cover

- 0 - 5 %
- 6 - 10 %
- 11 - 50 %
- 51 - 100 %

Pinyon-Juniper 5.5 million acres

Figure 3—(Continued).

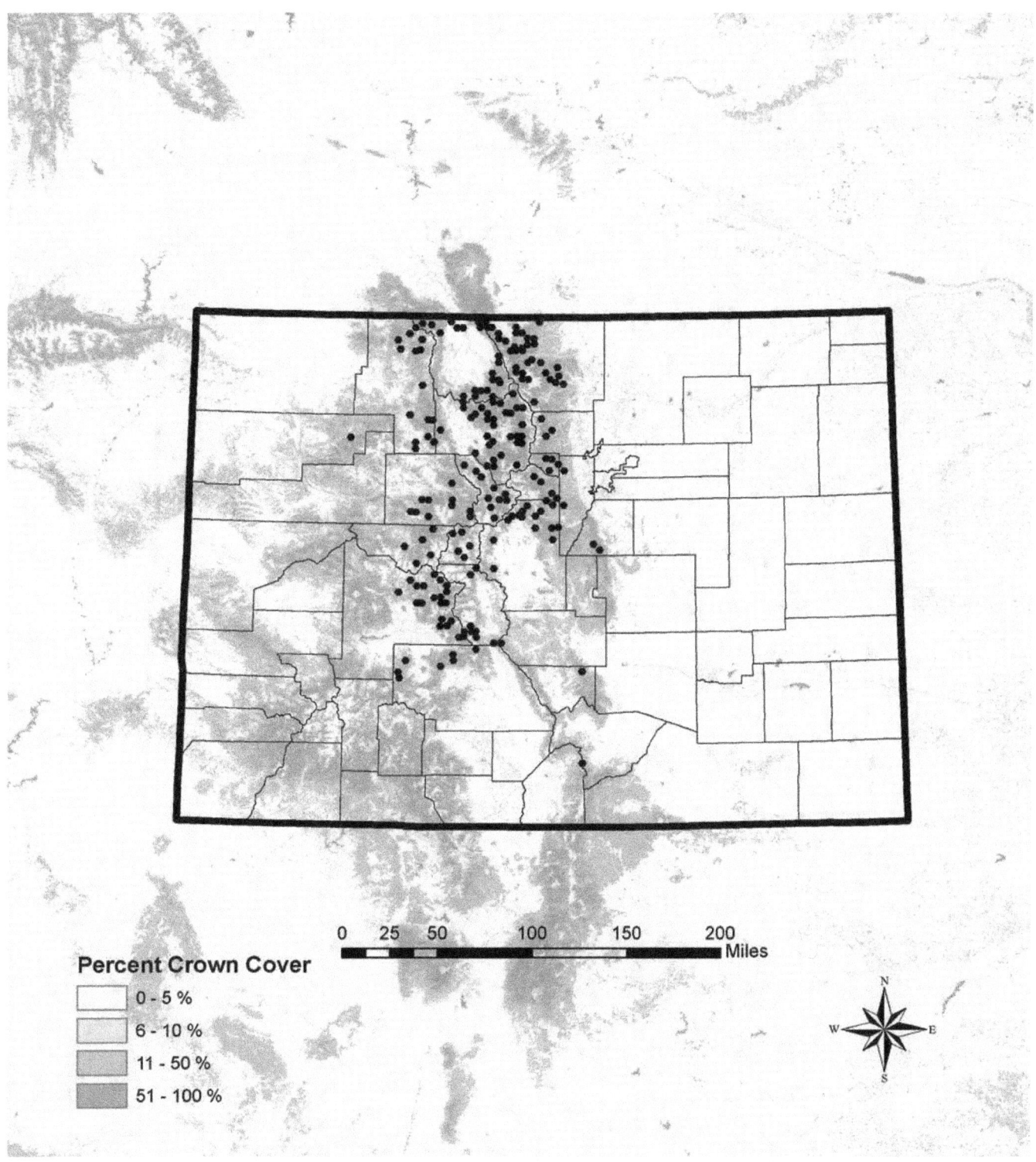

Lodgepole pine 2.1 million acres

USDA Forest Service Resour. Bull. RMRS-RB-11. 2010

13

Figure 3—(Continued).

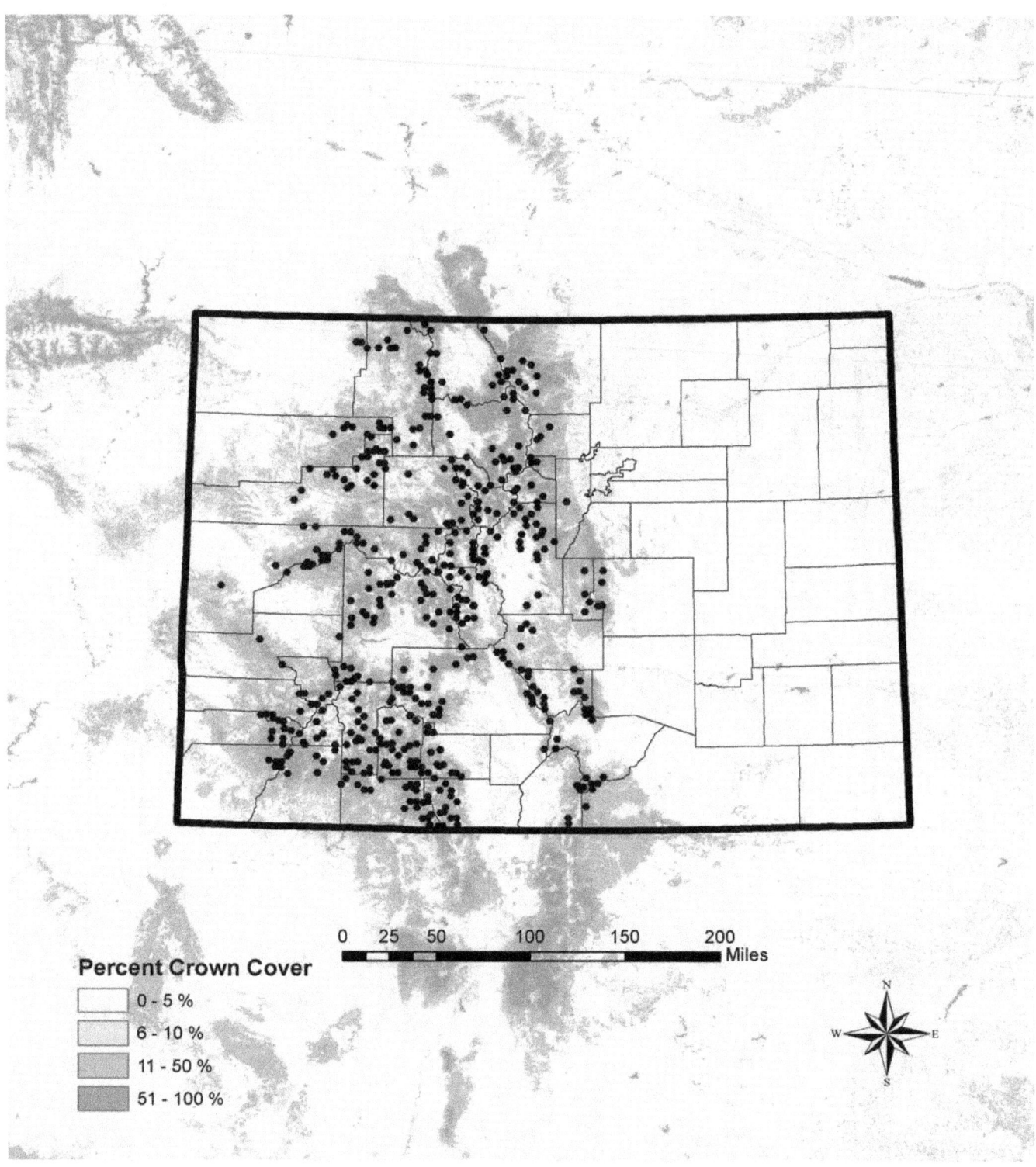

Fir-spruce-mountain hemlock 4.7 million acres

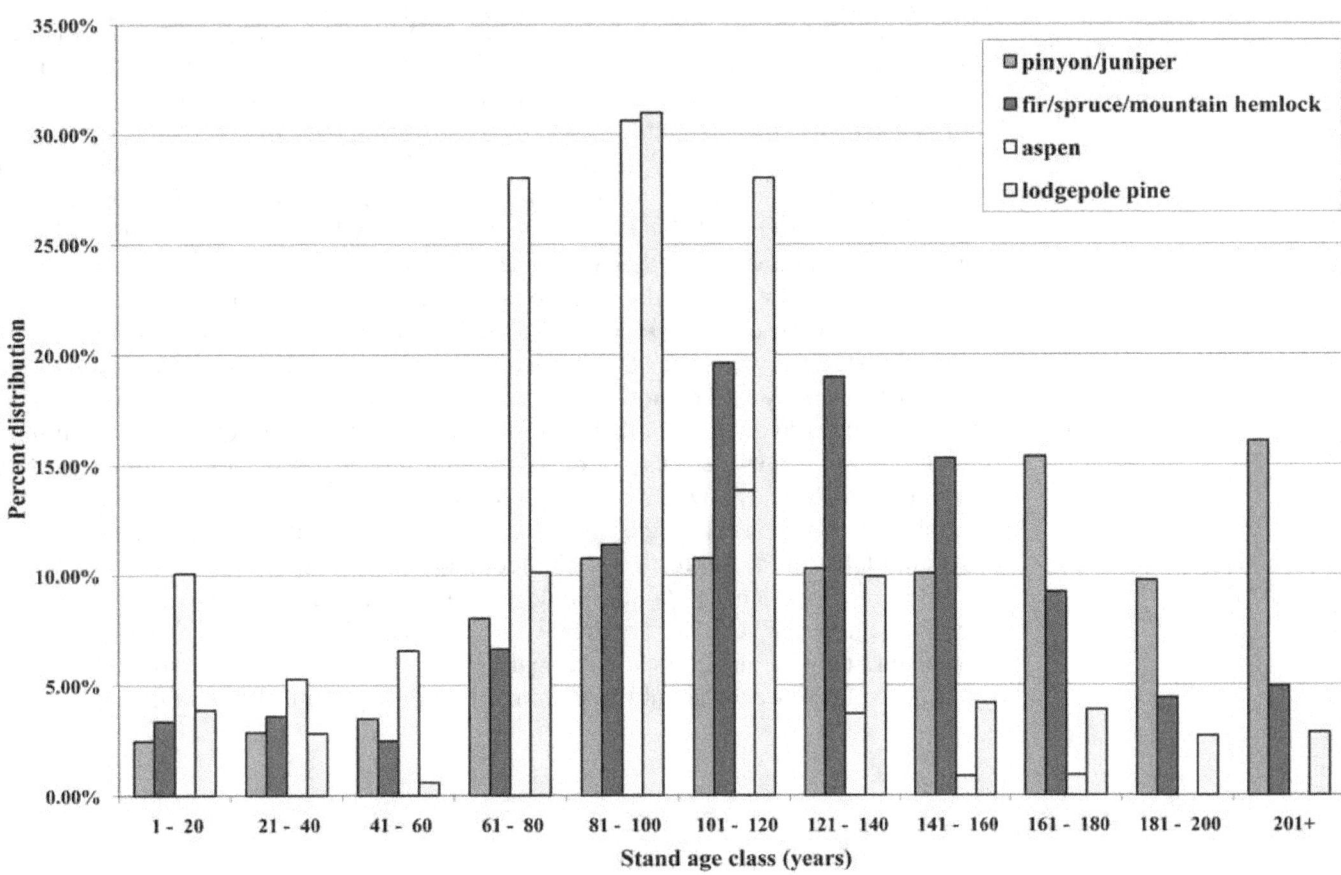

Figure 4—Distribution of forest land by stand age class and forest type group in Colorado, 2002-2006.

Stand Density Index (SDI)

Stand density index (Reineke 1933) is a relative measure of stand density, based on quadratic mean diameter of the stand and the number of trees per acre. In the western States, silviculturists often use SDI as one measure of stand structure to meet diverse objectives such as ecological restoration and wildlife habitat (e.g., Smith and Long 1987; Lilieholm and others 1994; Long and Shaw 2005).

SDI is usually presented as a percentage of a maximum SDI for each forest type (USDA Forest Service 1991). Maximum SDI is rarely, if ever, observed in nature at the stand scale because the onset of competition-induced (self-thinning) mortality occurs at about 60 percent of the maximum SDI. Average maximum density, which is used in normal yield tables and is equivalent to the A-line in Gingrich-type stocking diagrams (Gingrich 1967), is equal to approximately 80 percent of maximum SDI. There are several reasons why stands may have low SDI. Stands typically have low SDI following major disturbances, such as fire, insect attack, or harvesting. These stands remain in a low-density condition until regeneration fills available growing space. Stands that are over-mature can also have low SDI, because growing space may not be re-occupied as fast as it is released by the mortality of large, old trees. Finally, stands that occur on very thin soils or rocky sites may remain at low density indefinitely, because limitations on physical growing space do not permit full site occupancy. A site is considered to be fully occupied at 35 percent of maximum SDI. At lower densities, individual tree growth is maximized but stand growth is below potential, while at higher densities, individual tree growth is below potential, but stand growth is maximized (Long 1985).

Originally developed for even-aged stands, SDI can also be applied to uneven aged stands (Long and Daniel 1990; Shaw 2000). Stand structure can influence the computation of SDI, so the definition of maximum SDI must be compatible with the computation method. Because FIA data include stands covering the full range of structure, the maximum SDIs are currently being revised for FIA forest types (Shaw and Long, in preparation). The revised maximum SDIs, which are compatible with FIA computation methods, are shown in table E1. SDI was computed for each condition that sampled forest land using the summation method (Shaw 2000), and the SDI percentage was calculated using the maximum SDI for the forest type found on the condition.

The distribution of SDI values in Colorado is relatively balanced. Stands appear to be well-stocked, with over 60 percent of forest acres fully occupied (fig. 5). This distribution is likely to skew toward lower-density stands in the coming years, because the most recent data suggests that there has been considerable mortality in conifers. The data in this report reflect some of the drought-related mortality of common pinyon that started in 2003 (Shaw and others 2005), but there has been a dramatic increase in mortality in other conifer species in Colorado (see more information about conifer and aspen mortality in the "Forest Health" section of this report).

With time, low-density stands should increase in relative density due to growth of the residual trees. Whether or not there will be additional in-filling by regeneration will depend on a number of factors, including the timing of seed crops and favorable climatic conditions. These trends should be captured by future plot measurements.

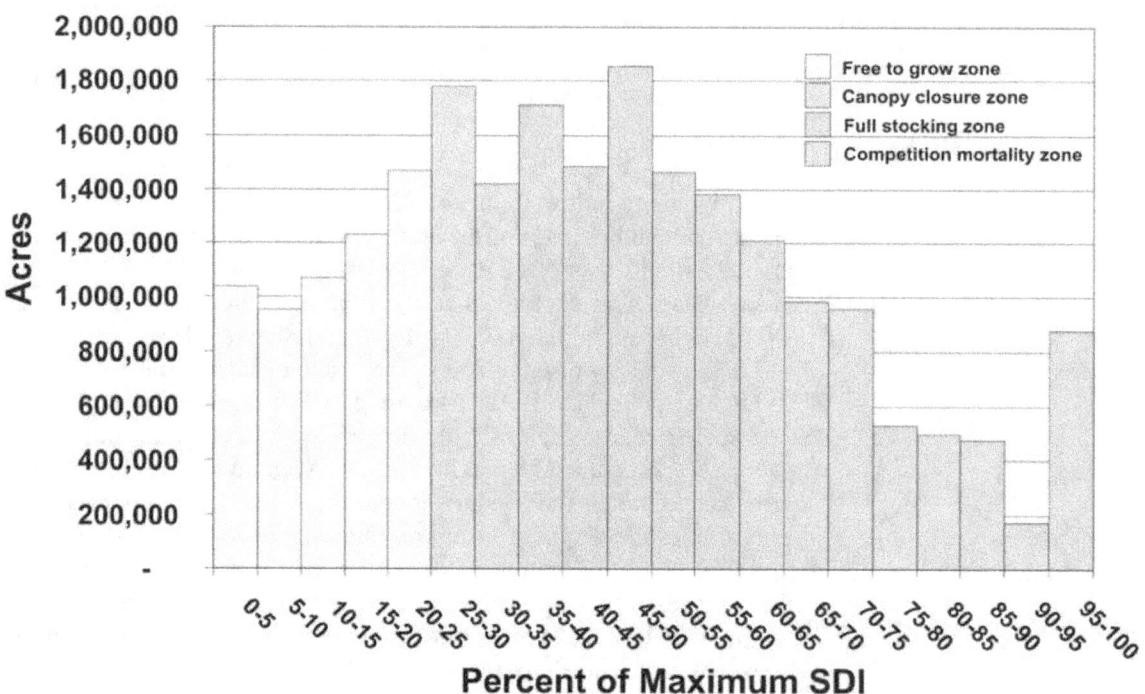

Figure 5—Distribution of stand density on forest land, Colorado, 2002-2006.

Numbers of Trees

A measure of the numbers of live trees is needed in a variety of silvicultural, forest health, and habitat management applications. To be meaningful, numbers of trees are usually combined with information about the size of the trees. Younger forest stands are usually comprised of large numbers of small-diameter trees whereas older forest stands contain small numbers of large-diameter trees.

There are an estimated 12.7 billion live trees in Colorado (table 10). Softwood species total 6.3 billion trees or 49 percent of the total (fig. 6). Over 54 percent of softwood trees are under 5.0 inches in diameter and nearly 6 percent are 15.0 inches and larger in diameter. The Engelmann and other spruce species group, comprised of Engelmann spruce and Colorado blue spruce, is the most abundant softwood species group accounting for 24 percent, or 1.5 billion trees, of the softwood total. Next in abundance is the true fir species group at 1.4 billion trees. The true fir species group is comprised of subalpine fir, white fir, and corkbark fir. Third in abundance is the western woodland softwood species group at 1.3 billion trees. The western woodland softwood species group is comprised of common pinyon, Utah juniper, Rocky Mountain juniper, and oneseed juniper. At 1.1 million trees, lodgepole pine is the fourth most abundant softwood.

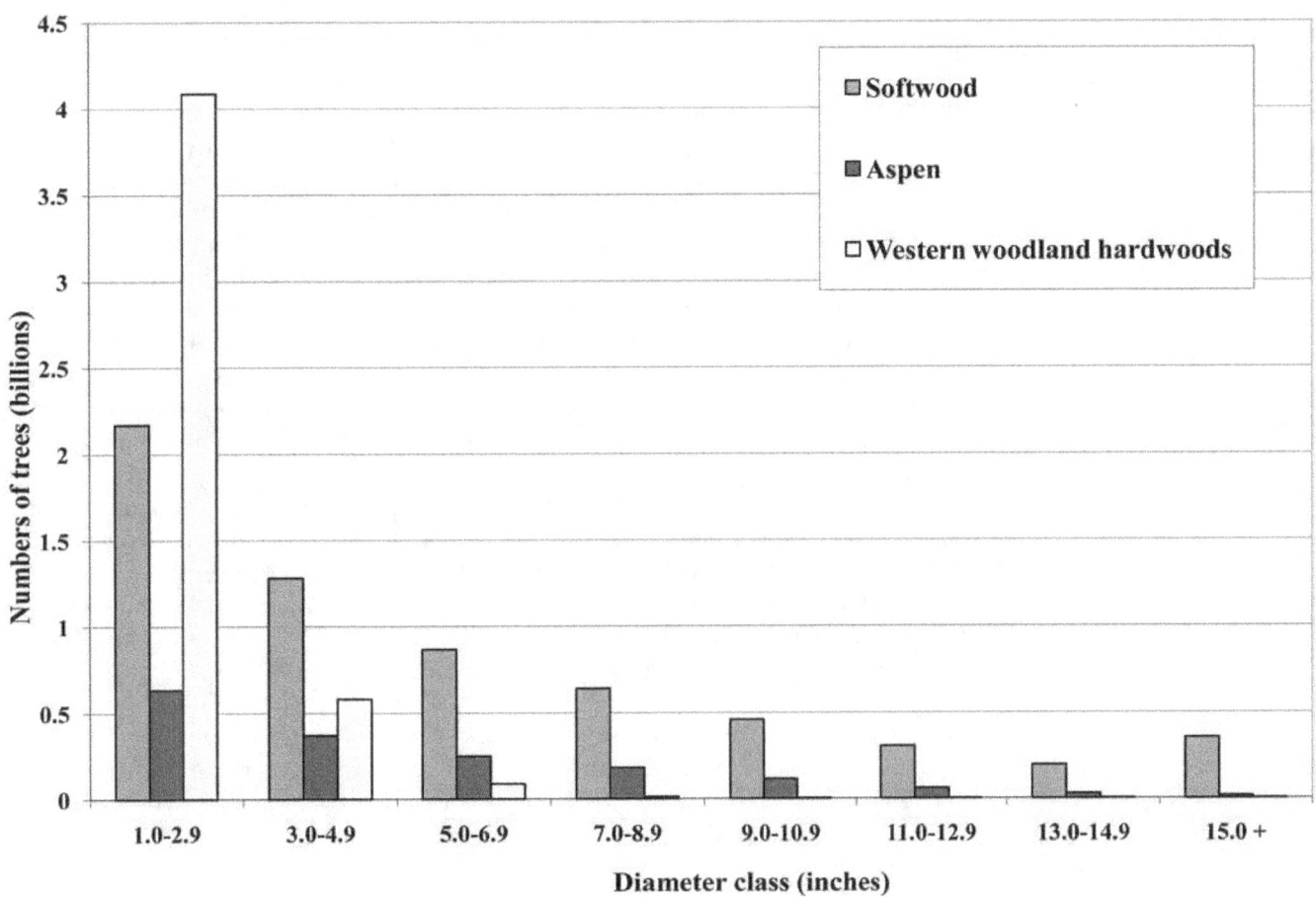

Figure 6—Number of live trees on forest land by species group and diameter class, Colorado, 2002-2006.

USDA Forest Service Resour. Bull. RMRS-RB-11. 2010

17

The western woodland hardwood species group accounts for the majority (74 percent) of the hardwood species occurring in Colorado. This species group is primarily gambel oak, a small, deciduous tree with a shrub-like growth form. The small-diameter characteristic is reflected in the size-class distribution of this species in figure 6. Nearly 98 percent of all western woodlan hardwoods stems are less than 5.0-inches in diameter.

Quaking aspen is a very important tree in Colorado. Stands of aspen are esthetically appealing and provide excellent habitat for a wide variety of wildlife. Numbers of aspen trees total nearly 1.7 billion making this species the single most abundant tree in Colorado. Most of the aspen trees are concentrated in the smaller diameter classes. Thirty-eight percent of all live aspen stems are in the 2-inch class and 49 percent are between 3 and 9 inches in diameter.

Live Tree Volume, Biomass, and Sawtimber

The amount of cubic-foot volume of wood in a forest is important for determining the sustainability of current and future wood utilization. The forest products industry is interested in knowing where available timber volume is located, who owns it, the species composition, and the size distribution. Biomass estimates are based on gross volumes; they exclude foliage and include all live trees 1.0 inches in diameter and larger.

The net volume of live trees in Colorado on forest land totals 37.3 billion cubic feet (table 12). Seventy-one percent, or 26.4 billion cubic feet, is located on lands controlled by National Forest System lands. Fourteen percent, or 5.3 billion cubic feet, is under private ownership. Thirteen percent, or 4.8 billion cubic feet is on lands controlled by various federal agencies not classified as National Forest System. The remainder, about 0.8 billion cubic feet, is on lands controlled by State and local government. The total weight of oven-dry biomass on Colorado forest land is 676 million tons.

Various factors affect whether timber is available for harvest. Three significant factors are ownership status, productivity, and merchantability standards. Timber volume on reserved forest land—land permanently reserved from wood products utilization through statute or administrative designation—is considered land that will not be harvested. Timberland is unreserved forest land capable of producing in excess of 20 cubic feet per acre per year of wood at culmination of mean annual increment. Forest land not capable of meeting this productivity threshold is assumed to have a low probability of being harvested. Historically, FIA has segregated live-tree volume based on growing-stock classification. Growing-stock trees are live trees that possess, or have the potential to produce an 8-foot sawlog that meets required merchantability standards (see "Standard Forest Inventory and Analysis Terminology" section). Therefore, the amount of growing-stock volume on timberland can be considered a reasonable benchmark for the amount of timber that is potentially available for harvest. Growing-stock volume on timberland in Colorado totals 25 billion cubic feet, or 67 percent of the total live volume on forest land (fig. 7). Net volume of sawtimber trees on timberland totals 92 billion board feet (table 19).

Engelmann and blue spruce together account for the majority (28) percent of growing-stock volume on timberland (fig. 8). Second in abundance, aspen totals 4.7 billion cubic feet of growing-stock volume. Growing-stock volume of lodgepole pine total 4.5 billion cubic feet and ranks third. The true fir species group ranks fourth at 3.3 billion cubic feet. Engelmann and blue spruce also account for the majority of sawtimber volume (32.5 billion board feet).

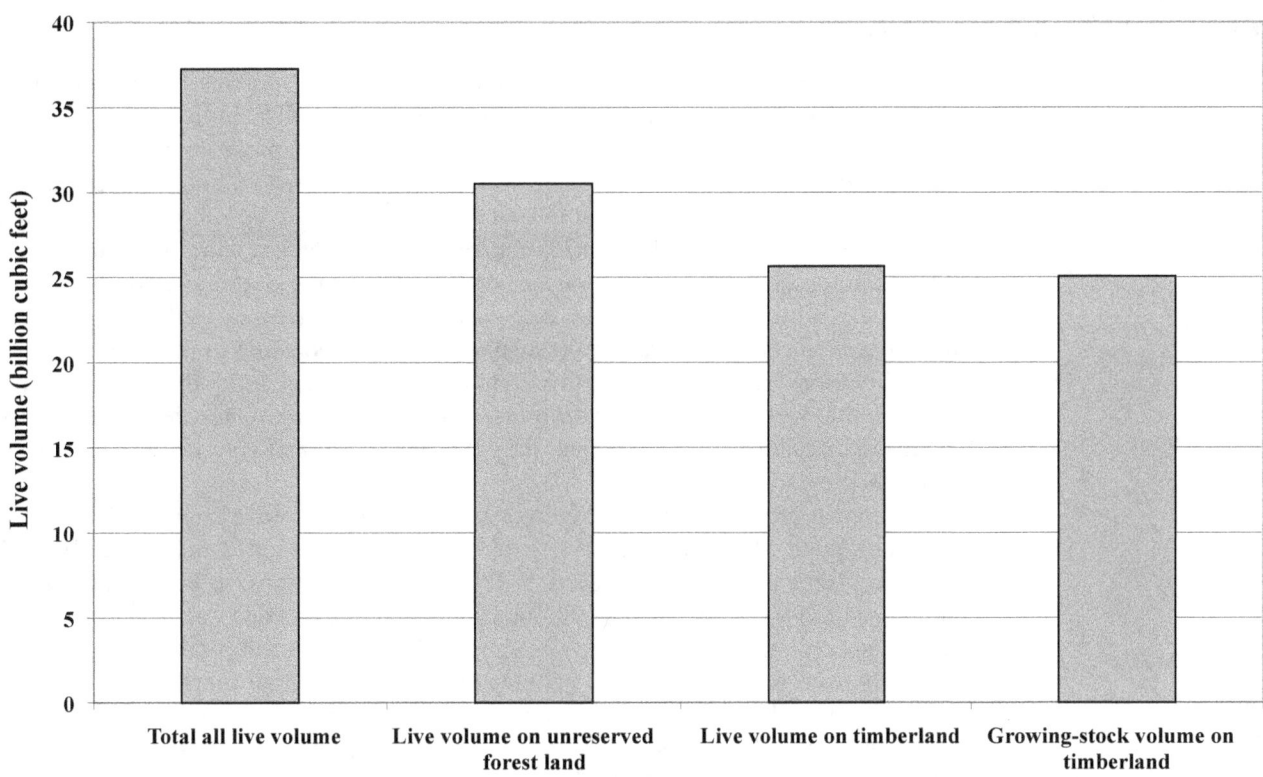

Figure 7—Volume of live trees on forest land by ownership status, productivity, and merchantability status, Colorado, 2002-2006.

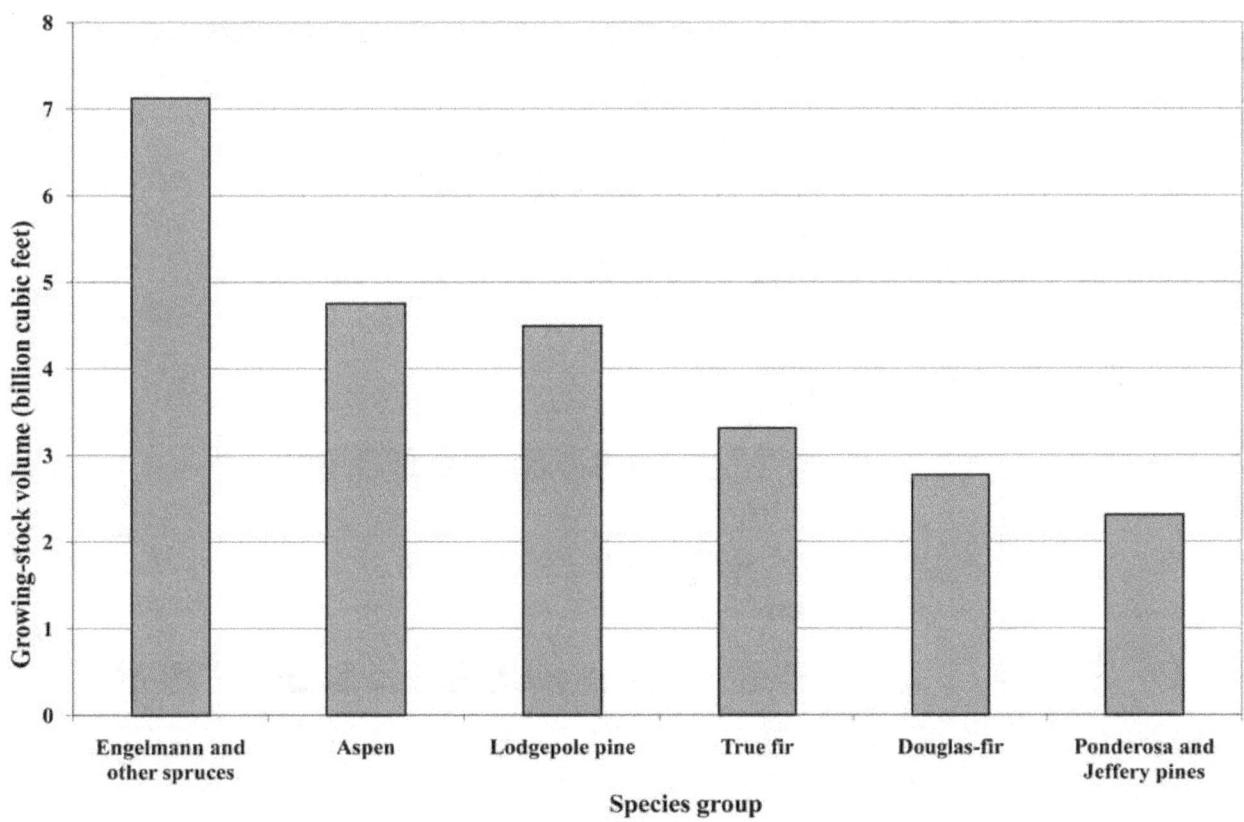

Figure 8—Volume of growing-stock trees on timberland by species group, Colorado, 2002-2006.

Forest Growth and Mortality

Two common measures of forest vigor and sustainability are tree growth and mortality. Growth, as reported here, is the average annual growth volume calculated from a sample of tree increment core measurements based on the previous 10 years of radial growth. Mortality, as reported here, is the average annual net volume of trees that have died in the 5 years prior to the year of measurement. The reason behind this growth and mortality estimation procedure in Colorado is that the inventory data are limited to initial plot measurements. Complete remeasurement data for the State—where the status of the plot and all trees on the plot are known at two points in time—will not be available until all ten panels of data are completed and remeasurement begins in the eleventh year.

The relationship between growth and mortality helps to quantify the change in inventory volume over time. Net growth minus mortality approximates the average annual change in inventory volume not including the average annual volume removed through timber harvesting (removals).

Net annual growth of all live trees 5.0 inches diameter and greater on Colorado forest land totaled 219.5 million cubic feet while mortality totaled nearly 421.0 million cubic feet (tables 22 and 25). Figure 9 illustrates the relationship between net growth and mortality by species group in Colorado. Mortality exceeded net growth for all major tree species except for aspen. The most striking relationship between growth and removals occurred in the true fir species group where annual mortality exceeded net growth by over thirteen-fold. Annual mortality of lodgepole pine was nearly five times net growth; mortality exceeded net growth by 11 percent for the Engelmann and other spruce species group. Aspen had the most positive relationship between net growth and mortality of any major species group in Colorado. Net annual growth of aspen exceeded annual mortality by 40 percent.

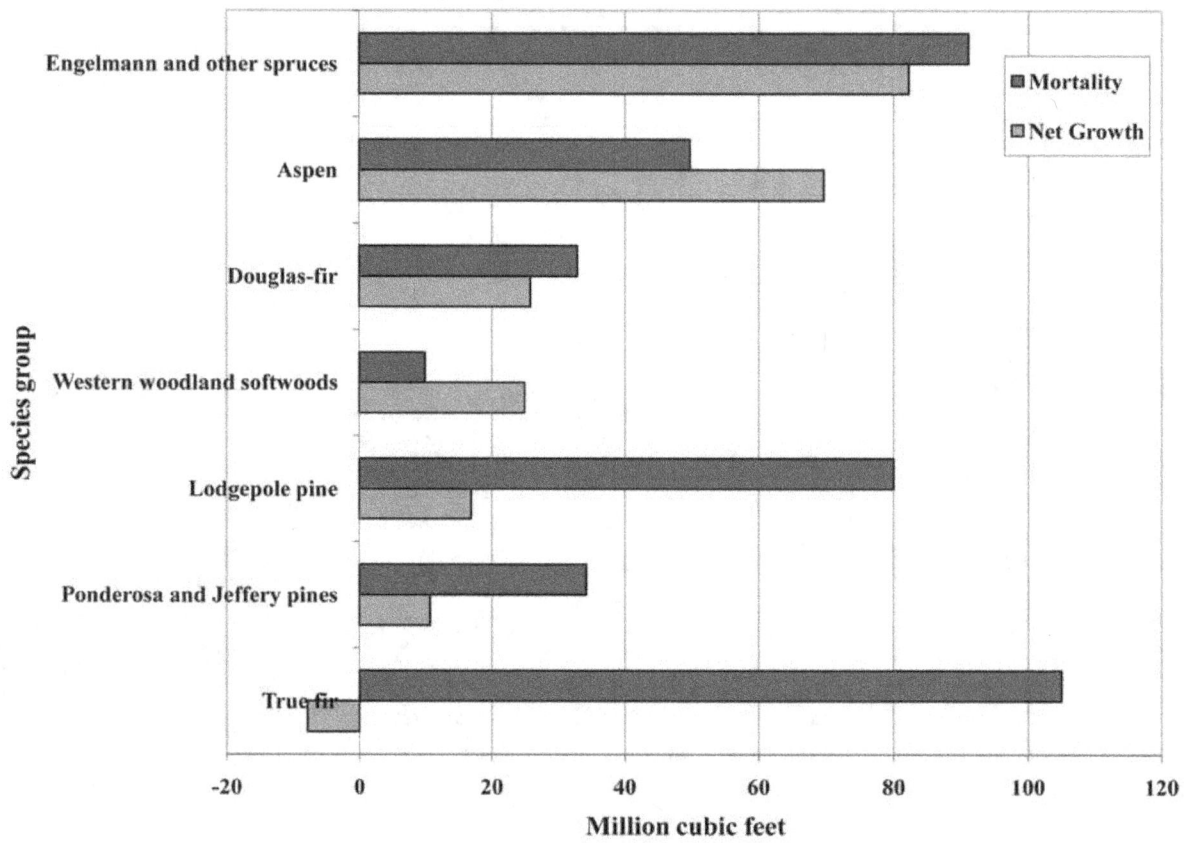

Figure 9—Net annual growth and mortality of live trees on forest land by species group, Colorado, 2002-2006.

Issues in Colorado's Forest Resources _____

Mountain Pine Beetle

The USDA Forest Service Region 2 Forest Health Management (FHM) Group began statewide aerial surveys of mountain pine beetle infestations in 1996. This monitoring effort has recorded significant increases in the area of lodgepole pine forests affected by the mountain pine beetle since 1996 and, as of 2007; the epidemic is believed to be catastrophic and unprecedented. Figure 10 illustrates a cartographic product produced by the FHM management center depicting the increase in area of lodgepole pine forests affected by the mountain pine beetle since 2002. The epidemic, which has caused widespread mortality of lodgepole pines in Colorado, may eventually alter the look of the landscape and presents a risk to local economies that depend on mountain tourism. Fire hazards, falling tree hazards, and threats to watersheds are some of the safety issues that have forest managers concerned.

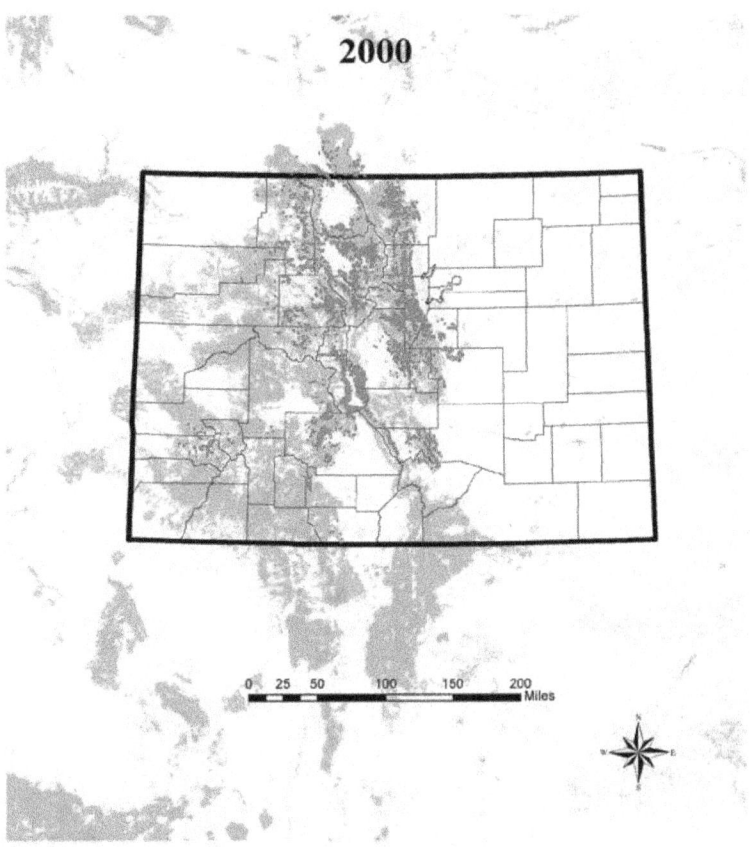

Figure 10—Epidemic spread of lodgepole pine tree mortality between 2000 and 2009 caused by mountain pine beetle in Colorado. Areas of heavy mortality are shaded red. These maps were created using digital coverage's downloaded from Forest Health Protection's Aerial Detection Dataset (USDA Forest Service, Forest Health and its Partners). The damaged areas were identified through aerial sketchmapping, which is a remote sensing technique that is independent of the FIA annual sample data. Land that has a minimum of 10 percent crown cover is shaded in green. More information about the Aerial Detection Dataset, aerial sketchmapping, and limitations associated with aerial survey data can be found at http://www.fs.fed.us/r2/resources/fhm/aerialsurvey/download/.

Figure 10—(Continued).

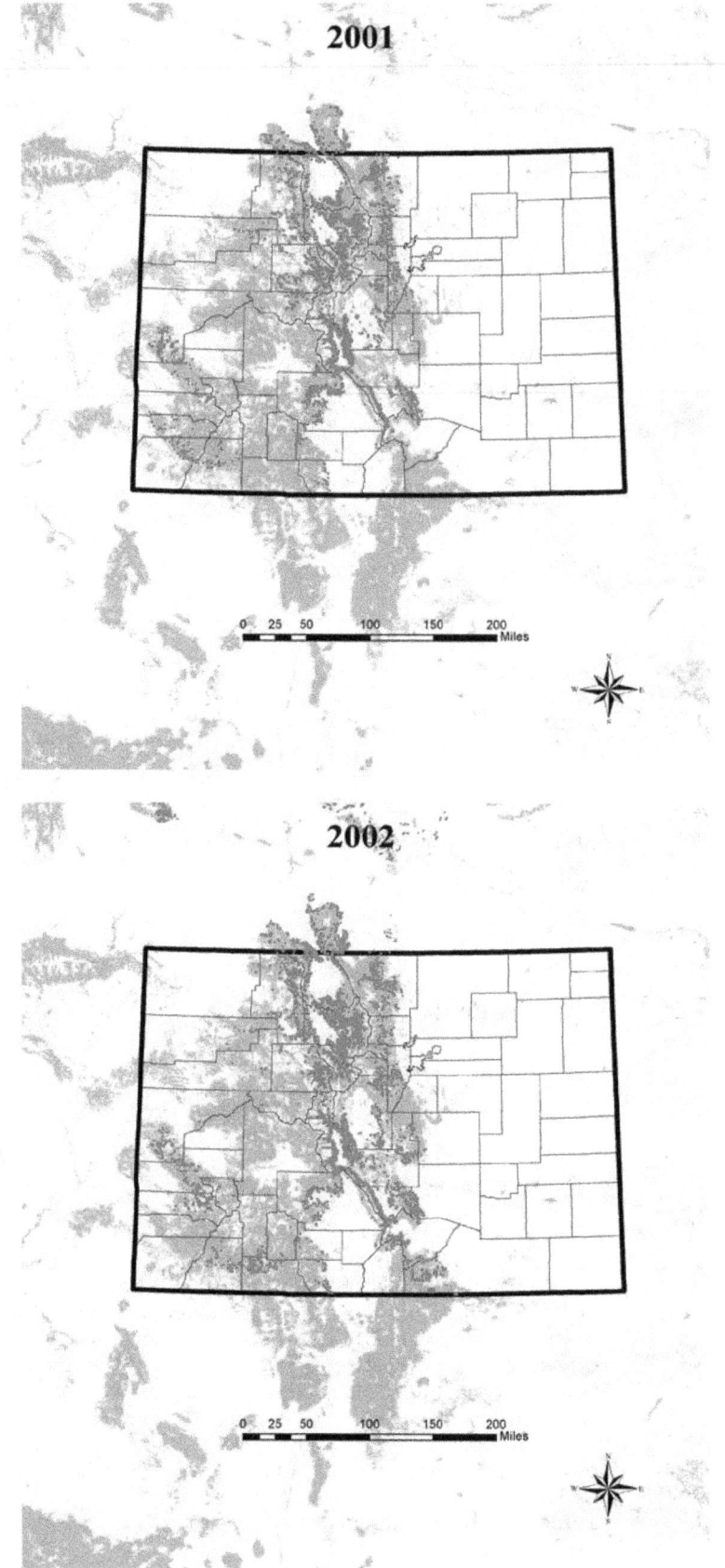

Figure 10—(Continued).

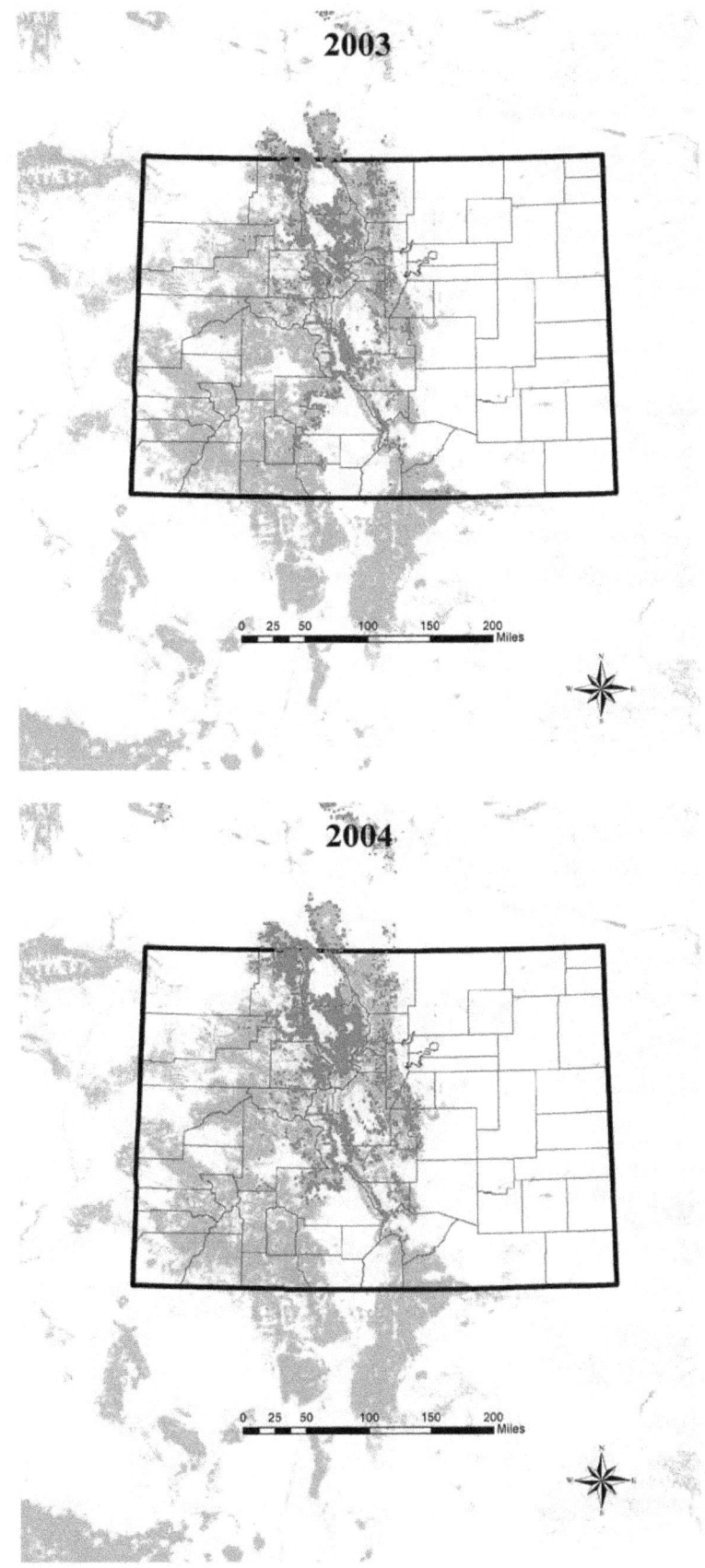

USDA Forest Service Resour. Bull. RMRS-RB-11. 2010

23

Figure 10—(Continued).

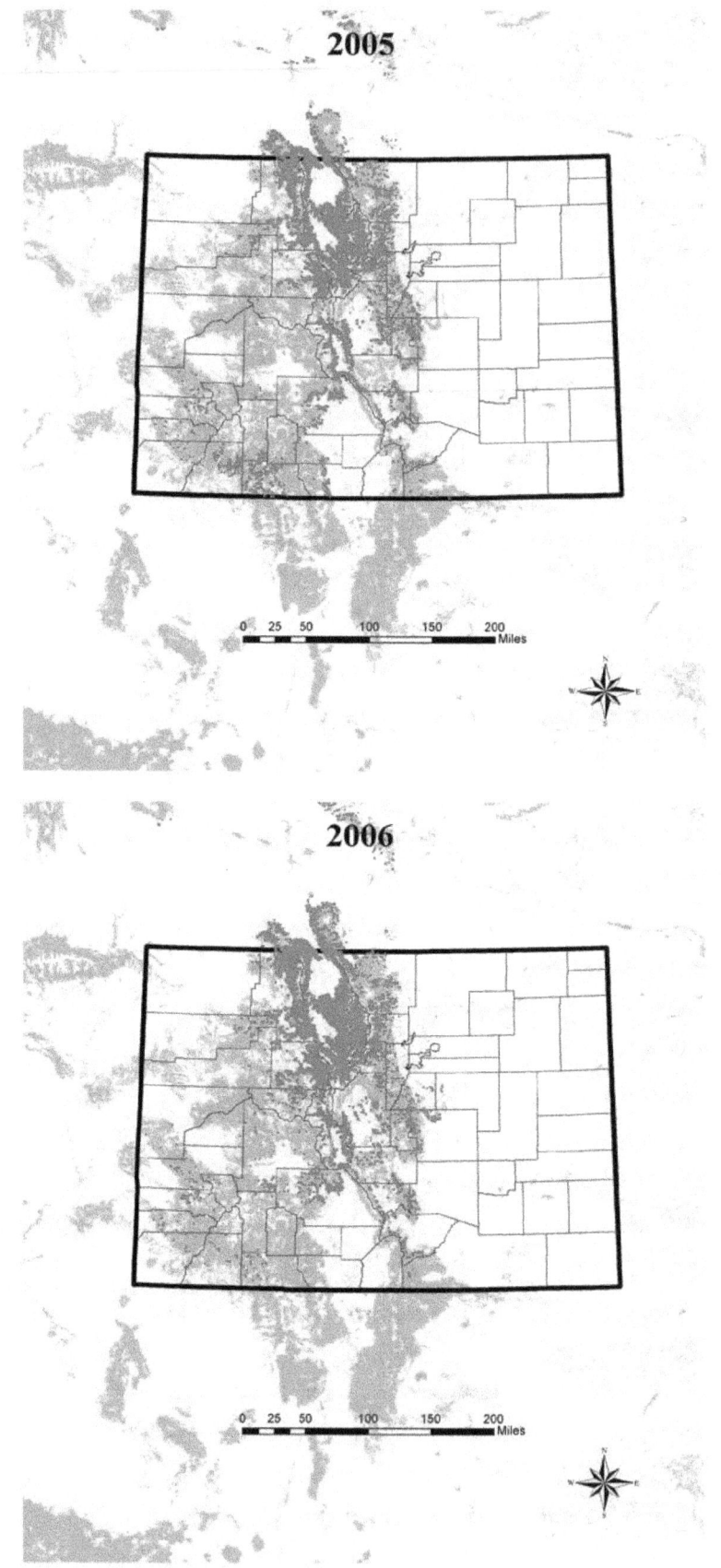

2005

2006

Figure 10—(Continued).

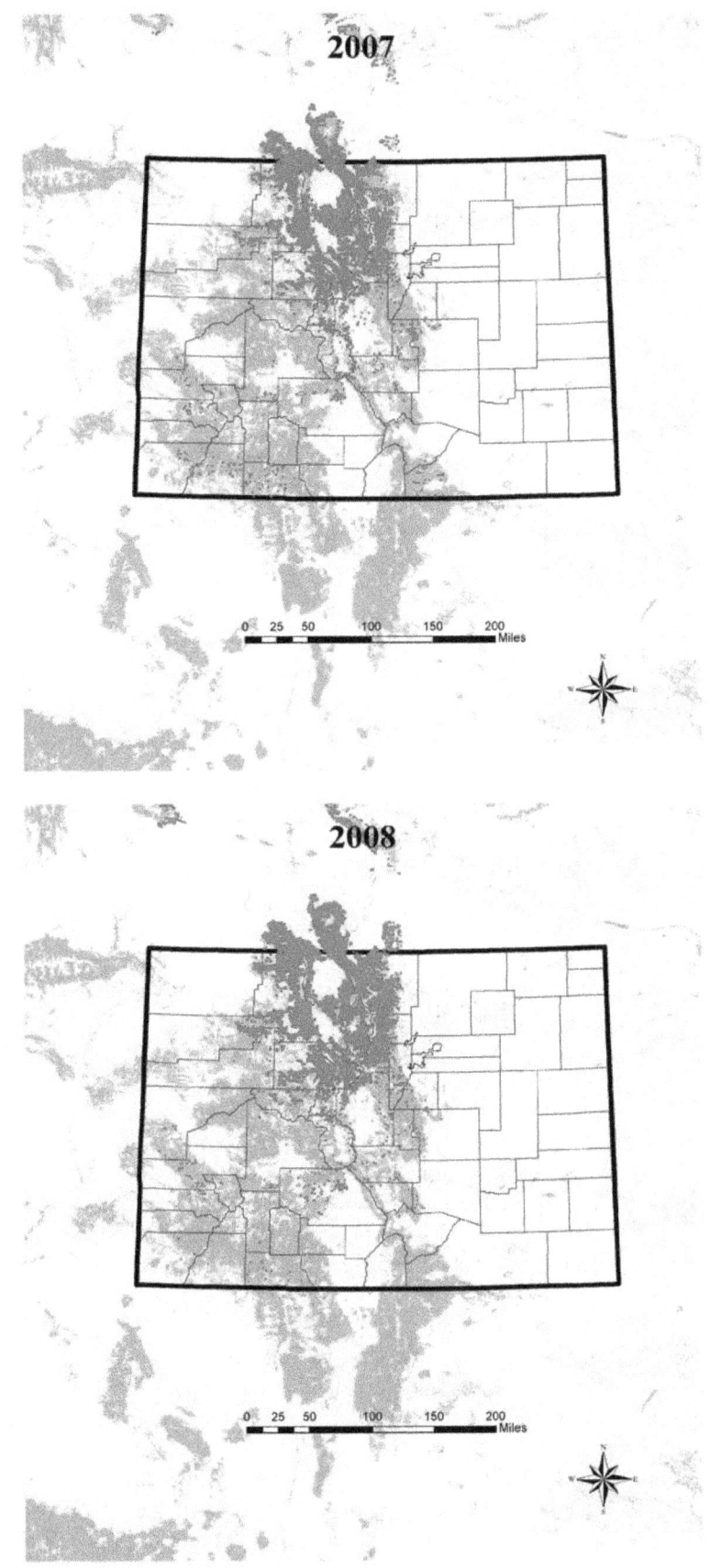

Figure 10—(Continued).

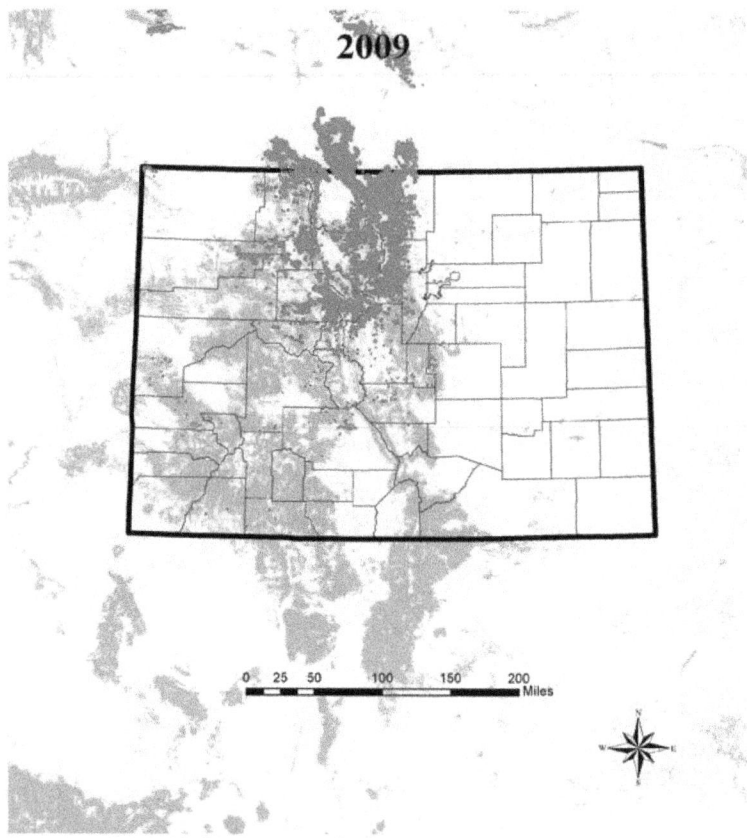

The mountain pine beetle is a native insect to western pine forests in North America and innocuous populations are almost always present in forests. Transition to epidemic populations is a function of the beetle's capacity to locate, colonize, and reproduce within suitable host trees in a weather pattern conducive to overwintering survival, emergence, and dispersal (Caroll and others 2004). The reasons behind the recent outbreaks have received considerable discussion. Most bark beetles prefer to invade trees that are in poor physiological condition (Rudinsky 1962). Temperature is known to influence insect outbreaks, especially species such as the mountain pine beetle (Amman 1973). Because of the recent interest in climate change, the effect of global warming is believed by some researchers to be a contributing factor in the severity of mountain pine beetle infestations (Logan and others 2003). Another significant factor is the presence of large areas of lodgepole pine stands comprised of ideal host trees homogeneous in age, composition, and structure.

Figure 11 illustrates the average annual biomass of lodgepole and ponderosa pine trees killed by insects by measurement year. The assumption is that most of the lodgepole and ponderosa pines classified as mortality and assigned a cause of death of insects is due to the mountain pine beetle. It is clearly evident that a pronounced upward trend has occurred during the 5 years of annual inventories in Colorado. As of 2006, the average annual biomass of insect-killed lodgepole pines is 926 thousand dry tons, which represents a nearly threefold increase over the 331 thousand dry tons recorded in 2002. Damage, and type of damage, is also recorded for all live trees 5.0 inches and larger on FIA plots. Figure 12 indicates the percentage of live lodgepole pines damaged by bark beetles by measurement year. The increase in percentage of lodgepole pine trees damaged by bark beetles reflects the increase in insect-killed trees. This percentage increased from 0.89 percent in 2002 to a high of 3.7 percent in 2006.

26

USDA Forest Service Resour. Bull. RMRS-RB-11. 2010

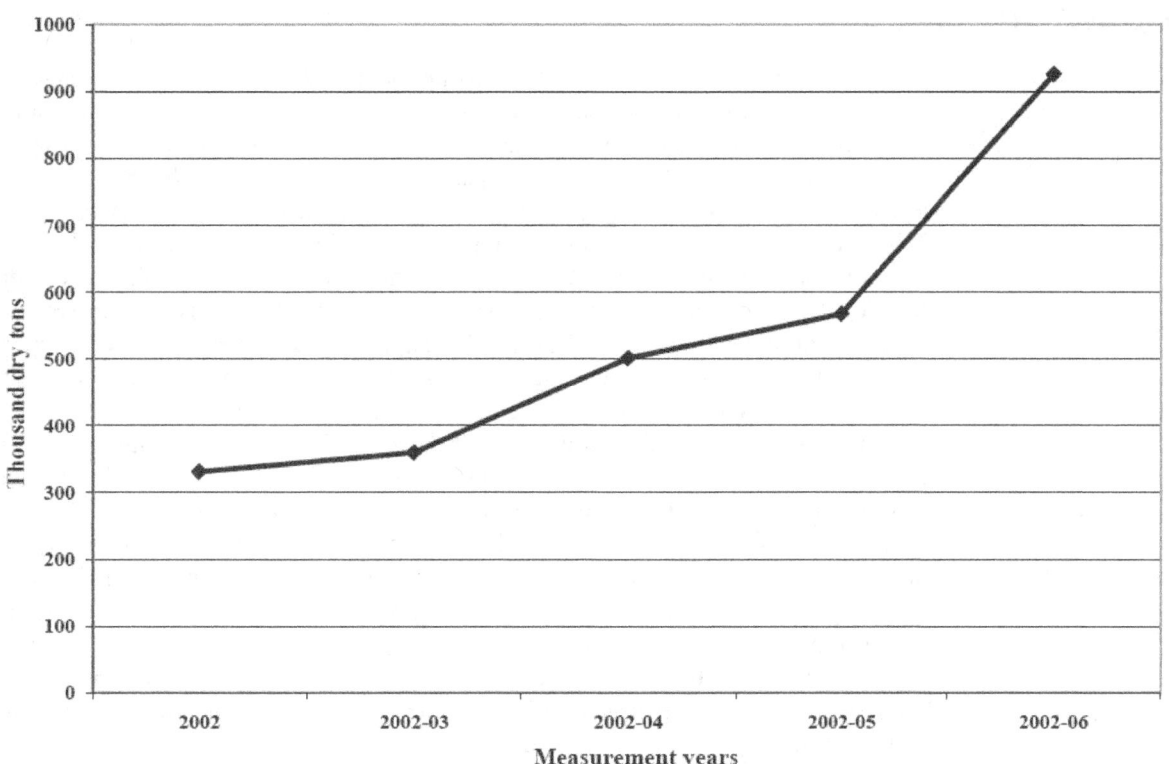

Figure 11—Moving average estimate of average annual aboveground dry weight of lodgepole and ponderosa pine trees killed by insects by measurement years, Colorado, 2002-2006.

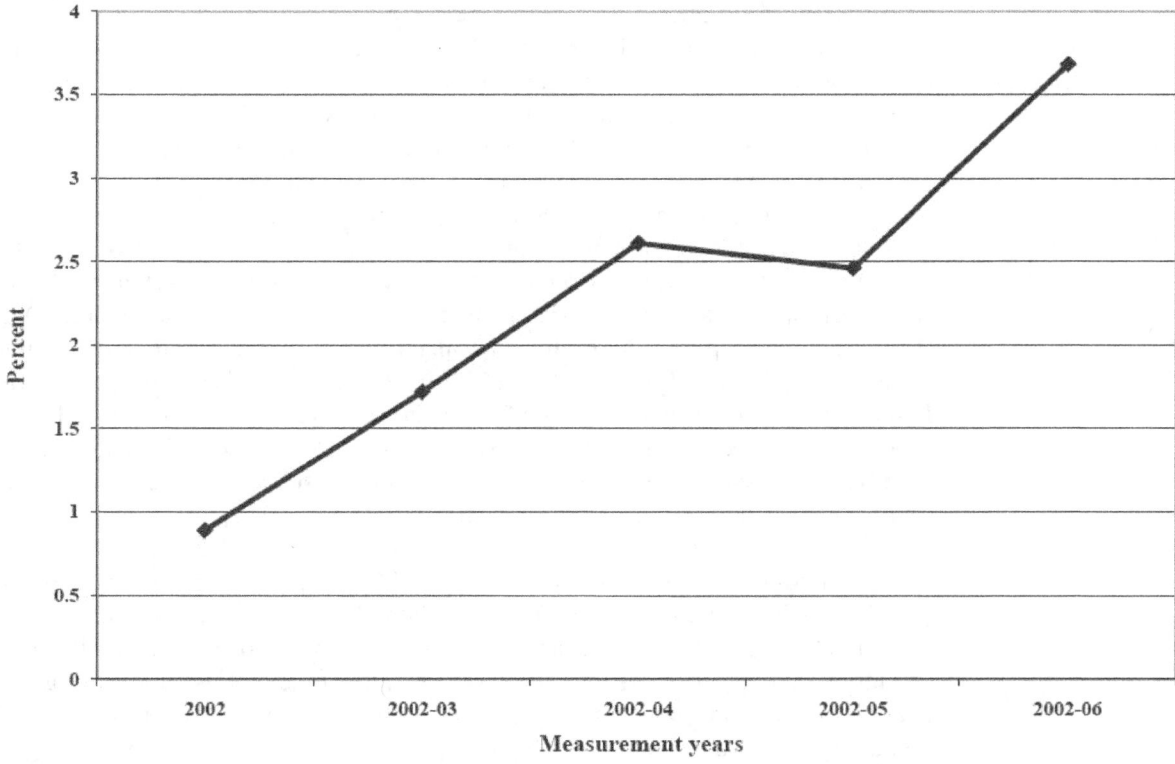

Figure 12—Moving average estimate of percentage of live lodgepole pines damaged by bark beetles by measurement years, Colorado, 2002-2006.

USDA Forest Service Resour. Bull. RMRS-RB-11. 2010

27

Sudden Aspen Decline

Quaking aspen is the most abundant and important hardwood species in Colorado. Aspen is a valuable ecological component of Colorado's landscape, occurring in pure forests as well as growing in association with many conifer species. In addition to the tree's desirable scenic value, the diversity of understory plants that occur under the aspen canopy supplies critical wildlife habitat, valuable grazing resources, and protection for soil and water.

Varied observers began noticing rapid mortality of aspen in multiple locales in southwestern Colorado beginning in 2004 (Worrel and others 2008). The difference between this recently observed aspen mortality and the typical mortality observed in aspen stands is the suddenness of the phenomenon and the apparent lack of regeneration occurring in stands where the overstory mortality is unusually high. Evidence to date suggests that it is a decline disease incited by acute, warm drought. Predisposing factors include low elevation, south and southwest aspects, droughty soils, open stands, and physiological maturity. The agents that actually kill the stressed trees include Cytospora canker, two bark beetle species, poplar borer, and bronze poplar borer.

How serious is the observed mortality of aspen? Unlike mountain pine beetle infestations, an event that has been extensively researched, there is no recorded precedent for this phenomenon. The aspen mortality appears to be a function of several agents acting singly or in combination. Aspen forests are dynamic and have always changed in response to climate, frequency and intensity of disturbance, and natural succession. No conclusive evidence to date indicates whether this event will continue or what the eventual impact on the aspen resource will be.

Figure 13 illustrates the average annual biomass of aspen trees classified as mortality by measurement year. All causes of death were included in this illustration. Unlike bark-beetle caused mortality in lodgepole and ponderosa pine forests, trends in aspen mortality over the annual inventory period in Colorado do not indicate a significant upward trend since 2002.

Aspen ecologists have also expressed concern about the level of aspen regeneration occurring in affected stands. In many of these stands, aspen sprouting is weak and the rootstock is in poor condition. For an aspen stand to successfully reestablish itself after a disturbance, sprouting must be abundant and vigorous to offset losses to ungulate browsing, diseases, and insects. Otherwise, other vegetative types may overwhelm the aspen component and the aspen clone will eventually die.

Is aspen successfully regenerating in Colorado? There are several ways that aspen regeneration can be evaluated using FIA data. Although aspen often grows in pure stands, the species also grows with a large number of other species such as Douglas-fir and lodgepole pine. Therefore, only analyzing plot data where forest conditions were classified as an aspen forest type eliminates many stands where aspen is present. Figure 14 illustrates the mean number of aspen trees on forest conditions defined as an aspen site. An aspen site is any forest condition where at least one live aspen (including seedlings), one standing dead aspen, or one aspen classified as mortality was recorded. The assumption is that these sites currently have or had the capability to support aspen. The number of live aspen seedlings on aspen sites average 690 stems per acre. Small diameter trees (1.0-4.9 inches d.b.h.) average 156 trees per acre, medium diameter trees (5.0-11.9 inches d.b.h.) average 79 trees per acre, large diameter trees (12.0 inches and larger) average 9 trees per acre, and aspen snags (standing dead trees 5.0 inches d.b.h. and larger) average 16 trees per acre. These mean numbers of aspen trees suggest that, overall, aspen stands have a distribution of trees sizes that do not indicate a significant deficiency in regeneration.

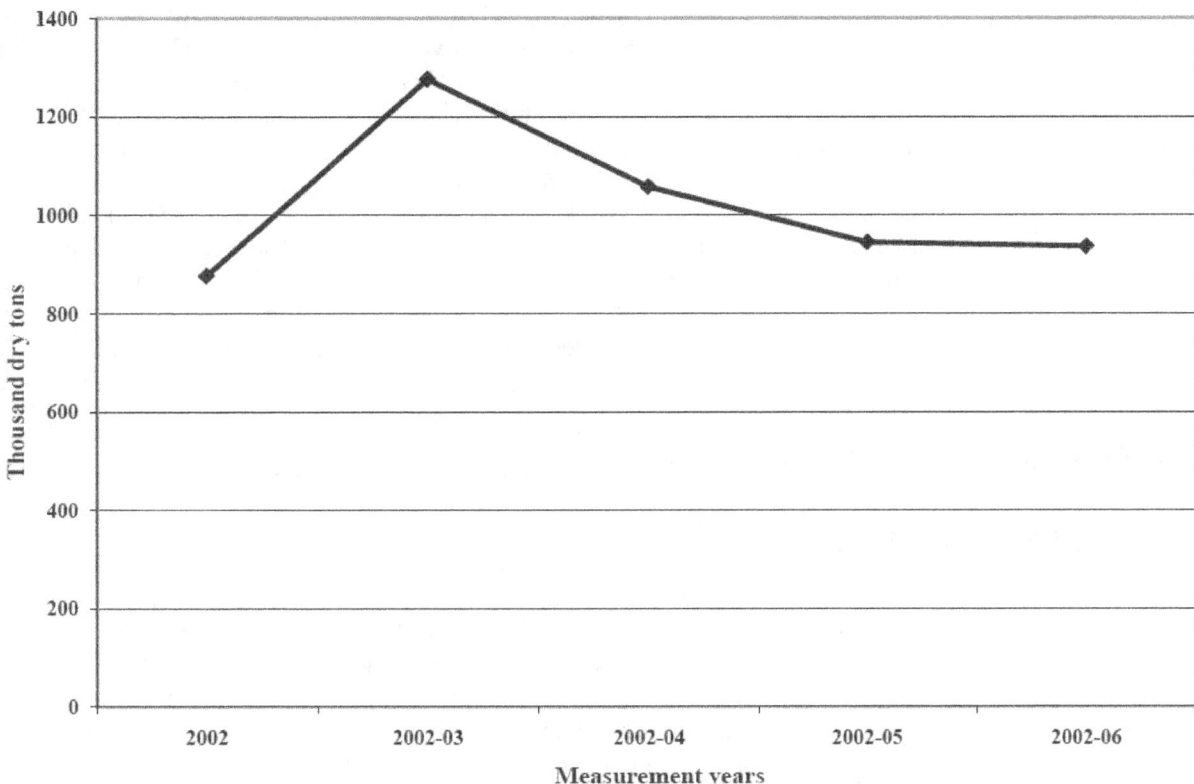

Figure 13— Moving average estimate of average annual aboveground dry weight of aspen trees classified as mortality by measurement years, Colorado, 2002-2006.

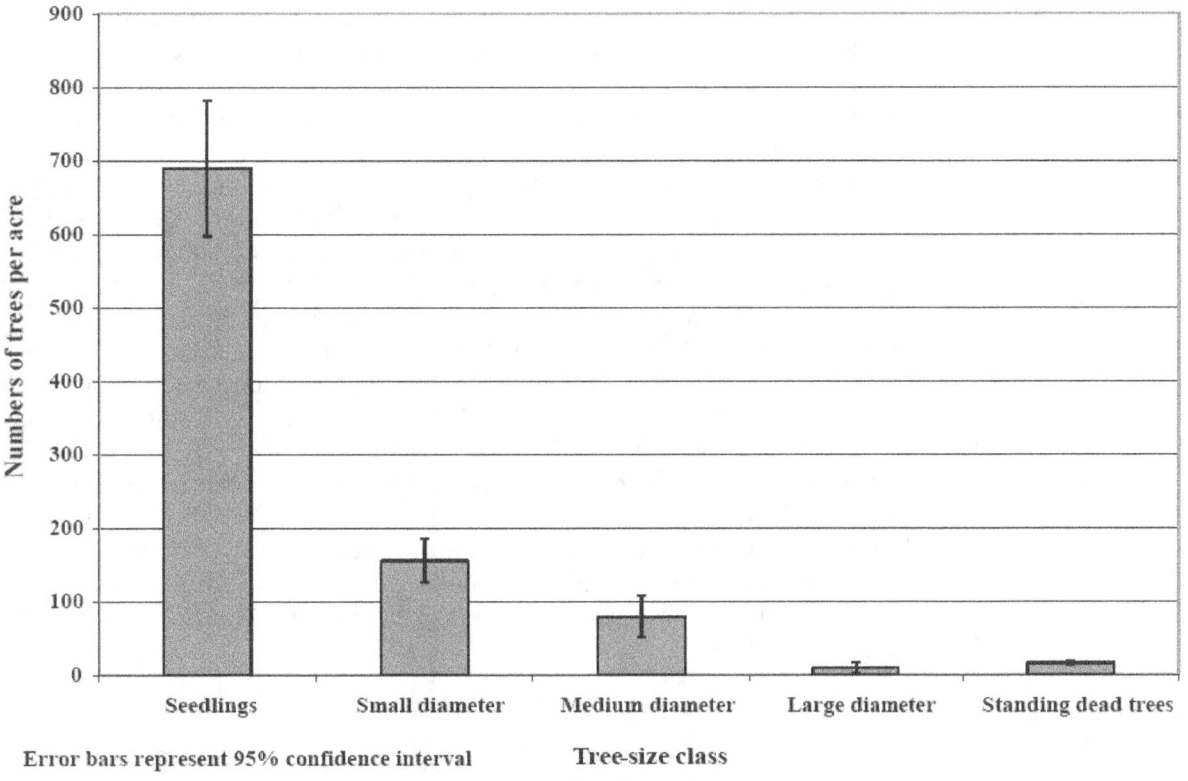

Error bars represent 95% confidence interval

Figure 14—Mean number of live aspen trees per acre on aspen sites by tree size class, Colorado, 2002-2006.

It does not appear that the recently observed aspen mortality event is reflected in Colorado's annual inventory. There are several reasons for this (Thompson 2009a). First, the rapid mortality associated with the phenomenon is relatively recent—it was first observed by researchers in 2004 (Worrel and others 2008). Second, it may be more of a localized event that will impact aspen in domains too small to be adequately captured in a broad-scale inventory. Third, the diverse factors associated with the decline make it difficult to assess cause of death and damaging agents that have been associated with the perceived decline. Fourth, aspen stands dynamics are complex. It is a relatively short-lived species susceptible to a host of pathological organisms. Aspen primarily regenerates through development of new shoots from the root systems of mature trees and successful regeneration depends on temperature, soil conditions, moisture, and age of parent trees.

Other Resources in Colorado's Forests

Invasive and Noxious Weeds

Noxious plant species can have many negative effects on forest communities. Invasive species can displace native flora, alter fire regimes, reduce diversity in the plant and pollinator communities, and generally reduce the diversity and resiliency of forest ecosystems. FIA field crews record any instance where a noxious weed is found on a plot that contains a forested condition. This allows for the spatial and temporal extent of these species to be documented as plots are revisited.

A total of 2,213 sample conditions were used to assess the occurrence of noxious plant species in Colorado. These samples represent plots that had a forested condition recorded somewhere within the boundaries of the four subplots. Thirty-three different weed species were documented on forested plots in Colorado, with one or more found on 384 (17.4%) of the sampled conditions. Cheatgrass (*Bromus tectorum*) and Canada thistle (*Cirsium arvence*) were the most common weeds species found. These two species accounted for just under 60 percent of the weed occurrences (fig. 15). Canada thistle was the most ubiquitous species, being detected on all forest-type groups other than Other Western Hardwoods.

The Elm-Ash-Cottonwood forest-type group has the highest infestation rate of at least one weed species, followed by the Nonstocked and the Ponderosa Pine groups respectively (fig. 16). Some of the forest-type groups have small sample sizes so results for these groups should be interpreted with caution. The Nonstocked group had the highest diversity of noxious species with eighteen, followed by the Aspen-Birch, Ponderosa Pine and Western Oaks groups which each had fourteen species (fig 16).

It appears that younger stands are more susceptible to infestation than are older stands. The sampled conditions that had stand-ages of less than 100 years were almost twice as likely to have noxious weeds found in them (fig. 17).

Colorado's forests appear to be susceptible to infestation of noxious species to varying degrees. While cheatgrass and Canada thistle were found in almost every type of forest, other species were more specialized or otherwise restricted to a handful of groups. The hardwoods tend to have a higher infestation frequency and a wider diversity of noxious species than the softwood groups, although the Ponderosa Pine group was an exception to this general trend.

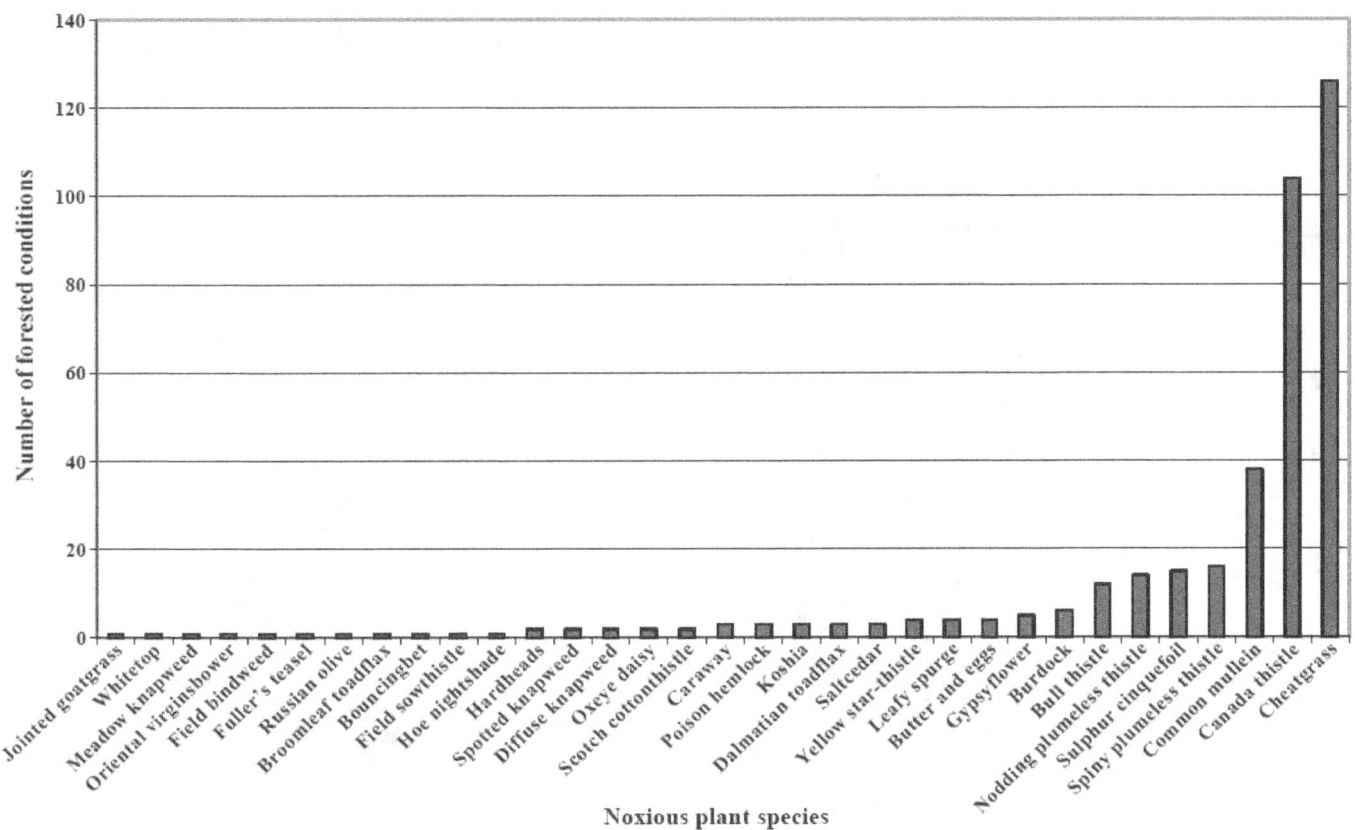

Figure 15—Frequency count of numbers of forested conditions with at least one noxious weed species present, Colorado, 2002-2006.

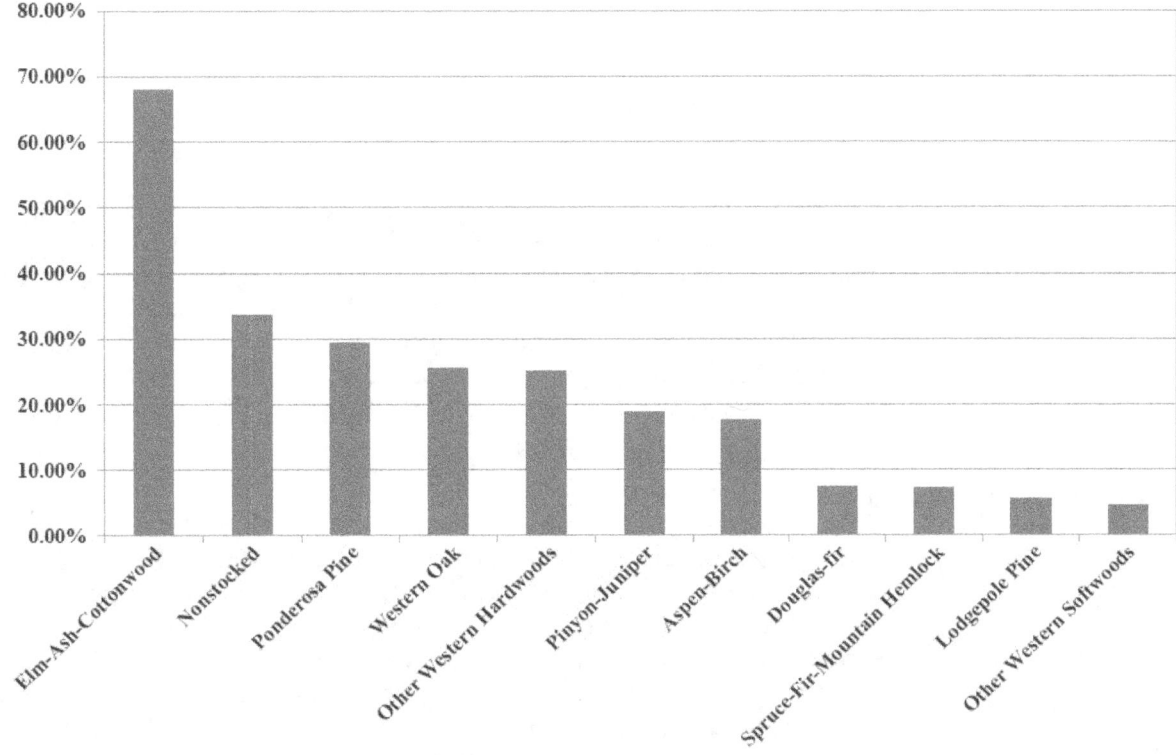

Figure 16—Percentage of plots infected with noxious weed species by forest-type group, Colorado, 2002-2006.

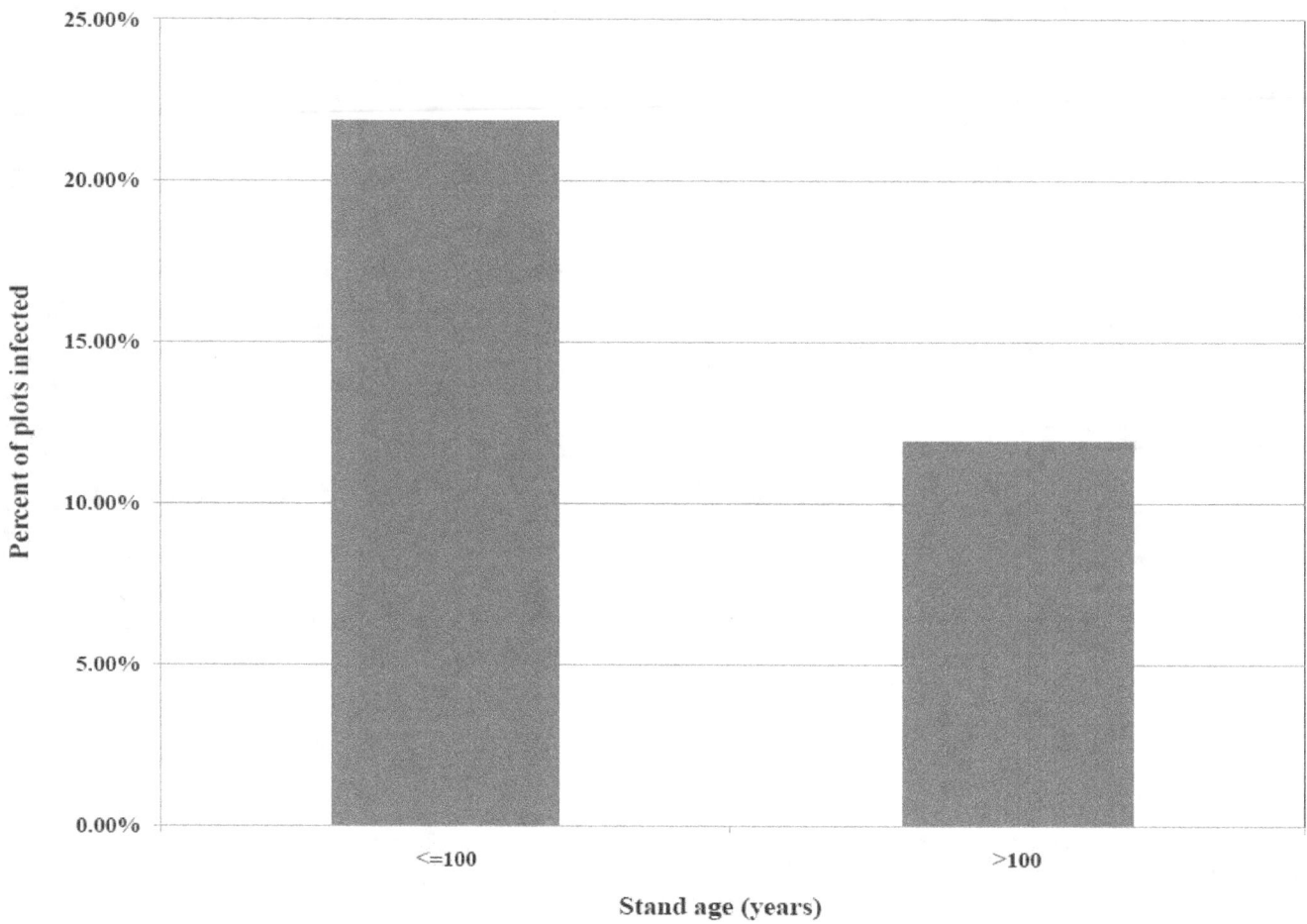

Figure 17—Percentage of forest conditions infected with noxious weed species by stand age, Colorado, 2002-2006.

Many nonstocked stands have recently been disturbed by fire, harvest, disease, or other perturbations that have removed much if not all of vegetative cover. These plots are more susceptible to invasion because noxious species can compete with native pioneer species for resources that were unavailable when the stand was stocked and had an established understory community. Understory communities are also still developing in young stands, leaving space and resources available for noxious species to utilize. More mature stands often reach a point of relative stability with native species using available space and resources.

Snags as Wildlife Habitat

Standing dead trees (snags) provide important habitat in the forested ecosystems of Colorado. There are countless organisms that utilize snags at some point in their life history. These include, but are not limited to, bacteria, fungi, insects, rodents, cavity-nesting birds, bats, raptors, mustelids, and black bear. The height and diameter of standing dead trees are important variables to species that consider the utility of snags as a nesting, roosting, or den site. Individual tree data collected by FIA field crews allow for population level analysis of the availability of and quality of individual snags that meet criteria important to wildlife.

USDA Forest Service Resour. Bull. RMRS-RB-11. 2010

Many of the species within the guild of cavity-nesting birds found in Colorado utilize snags that are greater than 9 inches d.b.h.. They also tend to choose trees 34 feet or taller when available. Silver-haired bats (*Lasionycteris noctivagans*) have been associated with trees 12 inches or greater d.b.h. and taller than 25 feet. Although black bears (*Ursus americanus*) do not require snags for den sites, pregnant females and those with cubs select them over ground dens where they are available. Bears prefer snags 30 inches or greater d.b.h. and taller than 16 feet. Examples below illustrate how FIA variables that record the d.b.h., actual height, live or dead status, and lean code can be used to quantify potential den, nest, and roost sites for black bears, cavity-nesting birds, and silver-haired bats.

There are almost 140 million snags in Colorado that meet the size preferences of most cavity nesting birds found in the State. Silver-haired bats have an estimated 74 million snags that have the potential to be suitable roost sites (fig. 18). There are roughly 766,000 trees that have the potential for black bear den sites in Colorado (fig. 19).

Available snags for cavity-nesting birds are predominately found in fir/spruce/mountain hemlock, aspen/birch and lodgepole pine forest type groups, but several other groups contribute potential habitat. These are the same forest types that hold the majority of snags preferred by silver-haired bats. However, the suite of forest type groups that have black bear den site potential is much smaller. Many snags usable as black bear den sites are found in the pinyon-juniper, fir-spruce-mountain hemlock and aspen/birch forest type groups.

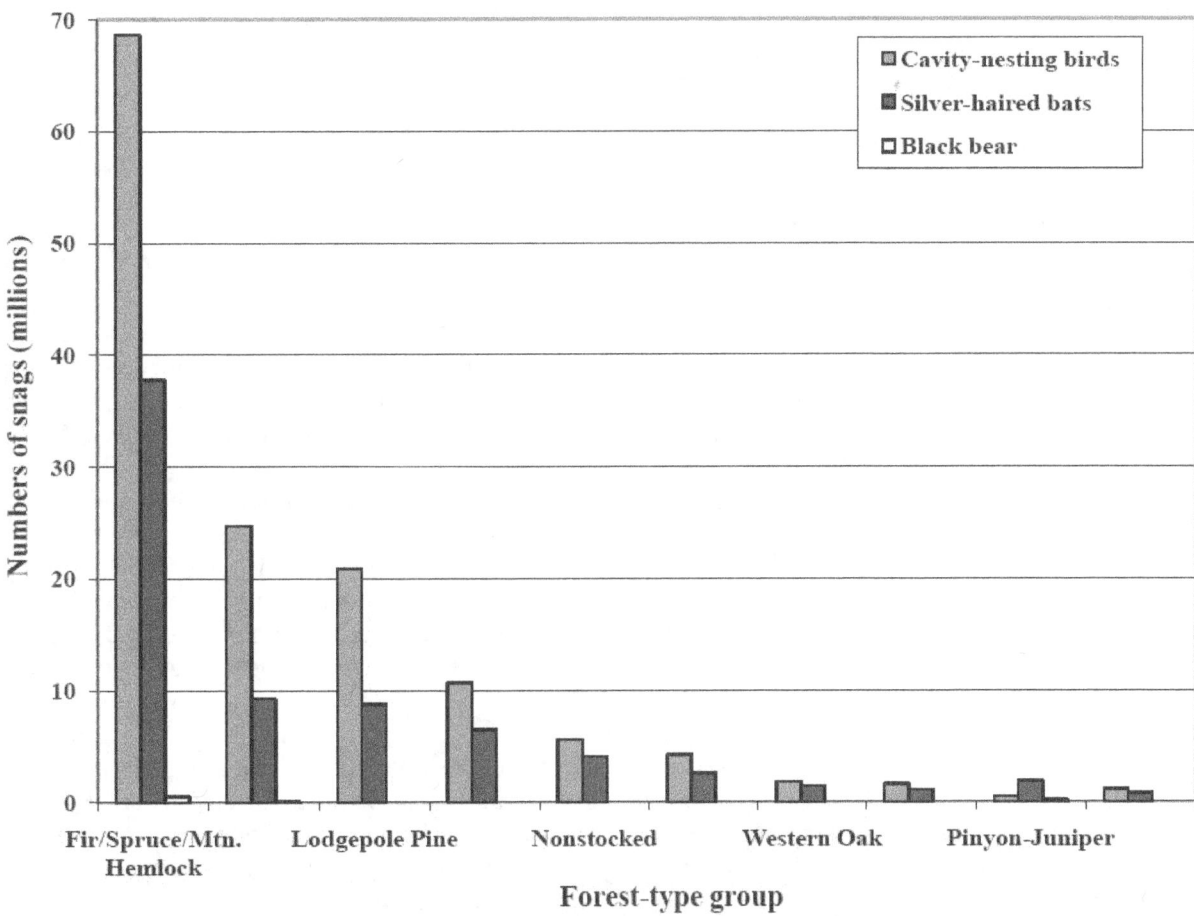

Figure 18—Number of snags that meet the size preferences of most cavity nesting birds and suitable roost sites for silver-haired bats by forest-type group, Colorado, 2002-2006.

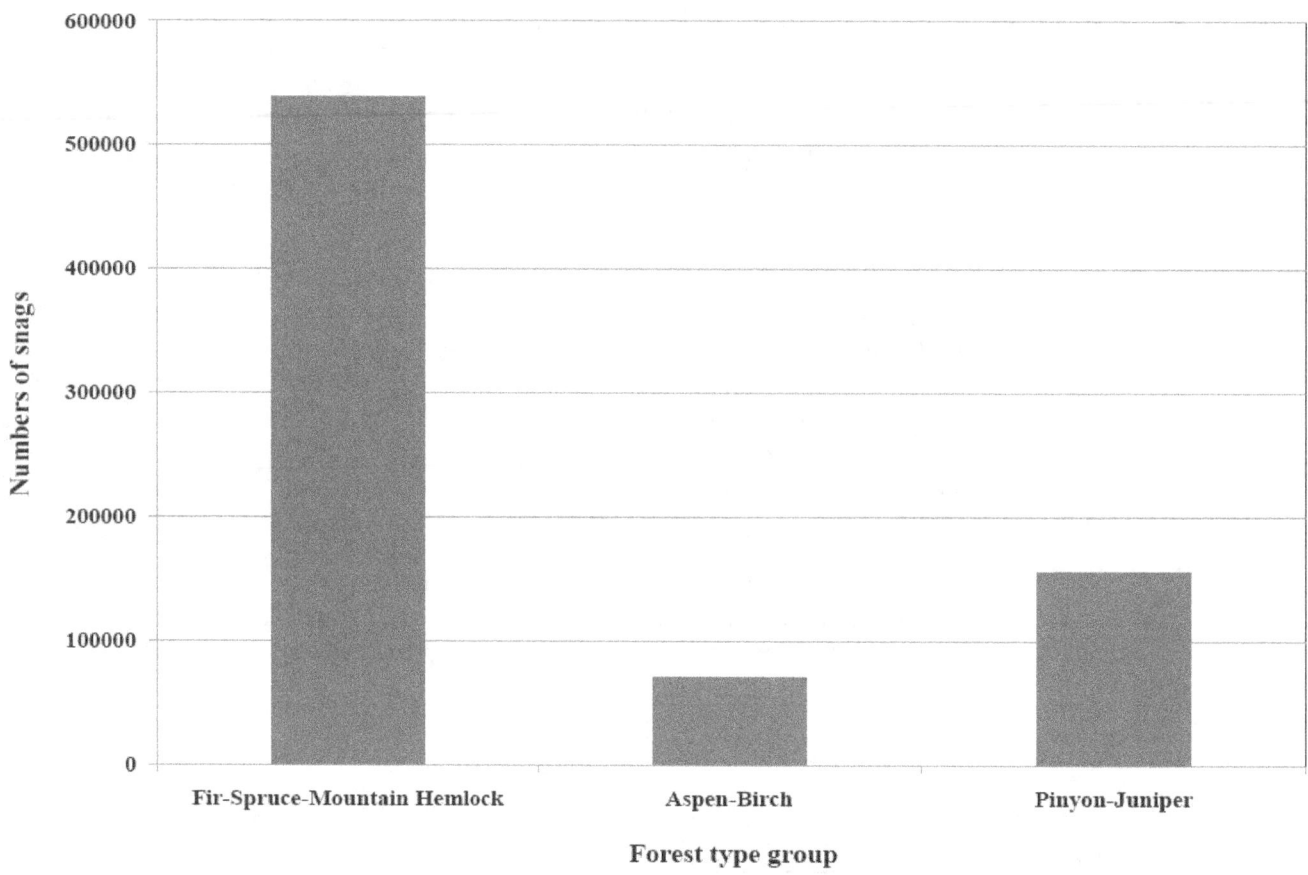

Figure 19—Number of snags that have the potential for black bear den sites by forest-type group, Colorado, 2002-2006.

Engelmann spruce contributes the most snags for all species combined, with subalpine fir, lodgepole pine and aspen being available in abundance for both bats and cavity-nesting birds (fig. 20). Engelmann spruce, Utah juniper and Douglas-fir provide the bulk of the potential den sites for black bear (fig. 21).

Aspen, Engelmann spruce, lodgepole pine, and subalpine fir are valuable tree species for several forest birds and mammals, even when found in other forest types (mixed stands). Depending on where they are located on the landscape, pinyon-juniper snags can be used by black bears. Variables other than snag dimensions and numbers need to be considered when predicting suitable wildlife habitat for forest-dwelling species. Proximity to forest edge and stand density of live trees is important to many cavity-nesting birds. The state of decay of a tree and its distance to water are important to silver-haired bats. Proximity to hard mast resources (juniper berries and acorns in Colorado), slope, aspect, presence of a cavity and the amount and timing of snow-pack are important in determining the relative value of trees as den sites for black bears. FIA data can address many of these factors and there are current efforts to build predictive models for these species in Colorado by using data collected by our crews. These models can be valuable tools for Federal and State land managers, as roughly 90 percent of the suitable snags measured by FIA occur on public lands.

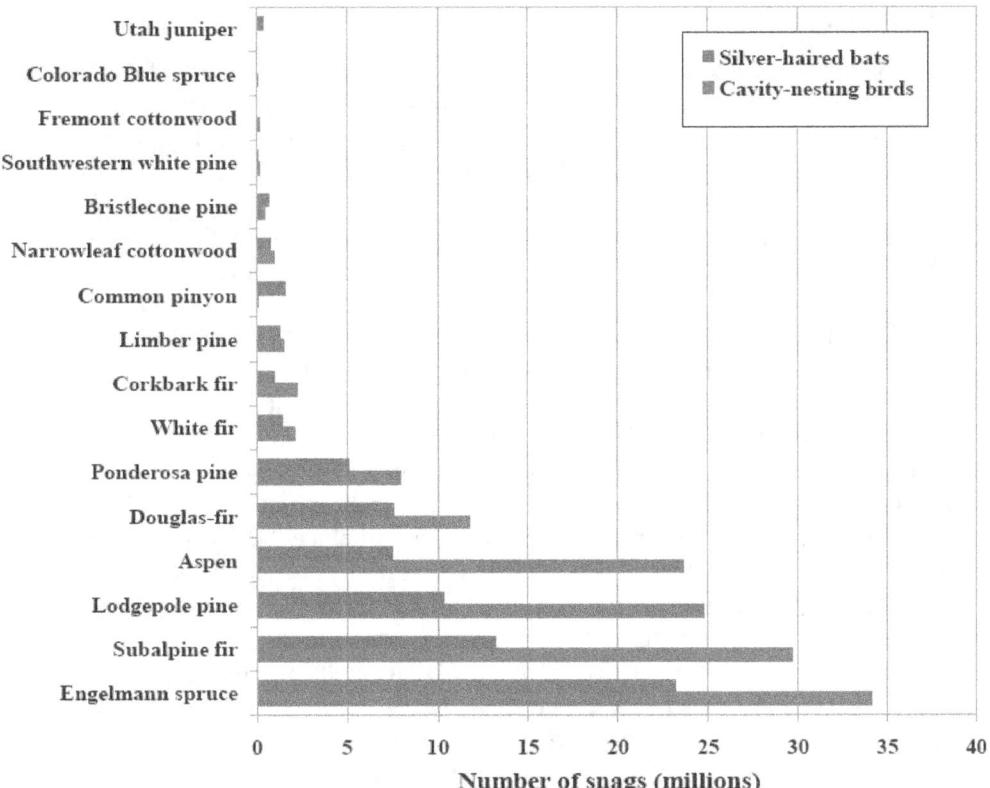

Figure 20—Number of snags that meet the size preferences of most cavity nesting birds and suitable roost sites for silver-haired bats by snag species group, Colorado, 2002-2006.

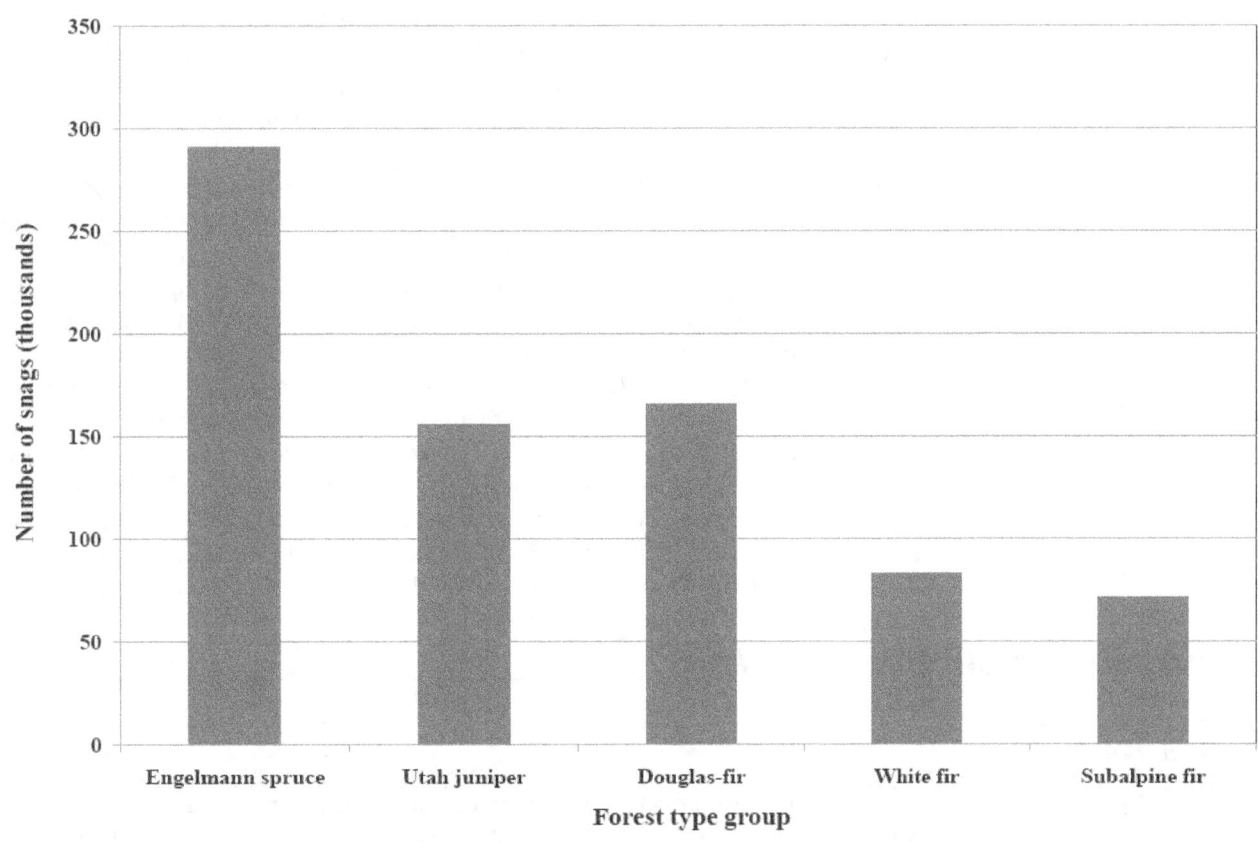

Figure 21—Number of snags that have the potential for black bear den sites by snag species group, Colorado, 2002-2006.

Forest Soil Resources in Colorado

Soils on the landscape are the product of five interacting soil forming factors: parent material, climate, landscape position (topography), organisms (vegetation, microbes, other soil organisms), and time (Jenny, 1994). Many external forces can have a profound influence on forest soil condition and hence forest health. These include agents of change or disturbances to apparent steady-state conditions such as shifts in climate, fire, insect and disease activities, land use activities, and land management actions.

The Soil Indicator of forest health was developed to assess the status and trend of forest soil resources in the United States across all ecoregions, forest types, and land ownership categories. For this report, data were analyzed and are being reported by forest type groups. This forest type stratification not only reflects the influence of forest vegetation on soil properties, but also the interaction of parent material, climate, landscape position, and time with forest vegetation and soil organisms. A complete listing of mean soil properties in Colorado organized by forest type is in the Soil Indicator core tables (tables E2, E3a, E3b, and E3c) in Appendix E. Some of the key soil properties were graphed by forest type group in Colorado, and to place these results in a regional context, these graphs are placed side by side with graphs of regional results.

With the exception of western oaks and western softwoods in Colorado, soil carbon and nitrogen percentages generally increased from drier to wetter forest environments in both Colorado and the Interior West region (fig. 22). Generally, soil moisture increases with elevation and latitude (cooler temperatures) and forest types reflect this climatic gradient. When expressed in terms of megagrams of carbon or nitrogen per hectare of forest area, carbon stocks also generally increase with elevation and latitude (fig. 23), with the exception of western oaks and western softwoods. Soil nitrogen stocks show a more mixed response to climatic gradients in Colorado and the Interior West.

Aspen forests store more N in the mineral soil than any other forest group in the Interior West (fig. 23, right side). In Colorado, both western oaks and aspen store the most soil nitrogen (fig. 23, left side). Aspen forests store significantly more nitrogen than spruce/fir forests, which often intermingle with aspen. High nitrogen levels in aspen forest floor and soils leads to lower carbon/nitrogen ratios than those found in forest floor and soils under spruce/fir (fig. 22). Since low carbon/nitrogen is a good indicator of relative organic matter decomposition rate, nutrient-rich aspen leaves decompose quickly and easily compared to spruce/fir needles.

Soil pH generally decreases with increasing elevation, latitude, and precipitation (fig. 24). The more acidic soils are found in the wetter high-elevation forest types. This is also reflected in higher levels of exchangeable Al in wetter high-elevation forest soils (fig. 24). In both Colorado and the Interior West as a whole, much higher levels of aluminum are found in spruce/fir than aspen soils. Aspen are intolerant of high levels of exchangeable aluminum. In the Interior West as a whole, aspen soils store more potassium than other forest type groups (fig. 24). In Colorado, western oaks, Douglas fir, aspen, and some western softwoods forests store comparable amounts of soil potassium. High levels of exchangeable calcium are found in the calcareous, high-pH soils under western hardwoods including oaks and pinyon/juniper group woodlands (fig. 24).

Removals for Timber Products _____

Background

Volume removed from forest inventory during the harvesting of timber is known as removals. Removals are an important indicator of the sustainability of timber harvest. Removals that exceed growth could indicate over-harvesting and decreasing forest

36

USDA Forest Service Resour. Bull. RMRS-RB-11. 2010

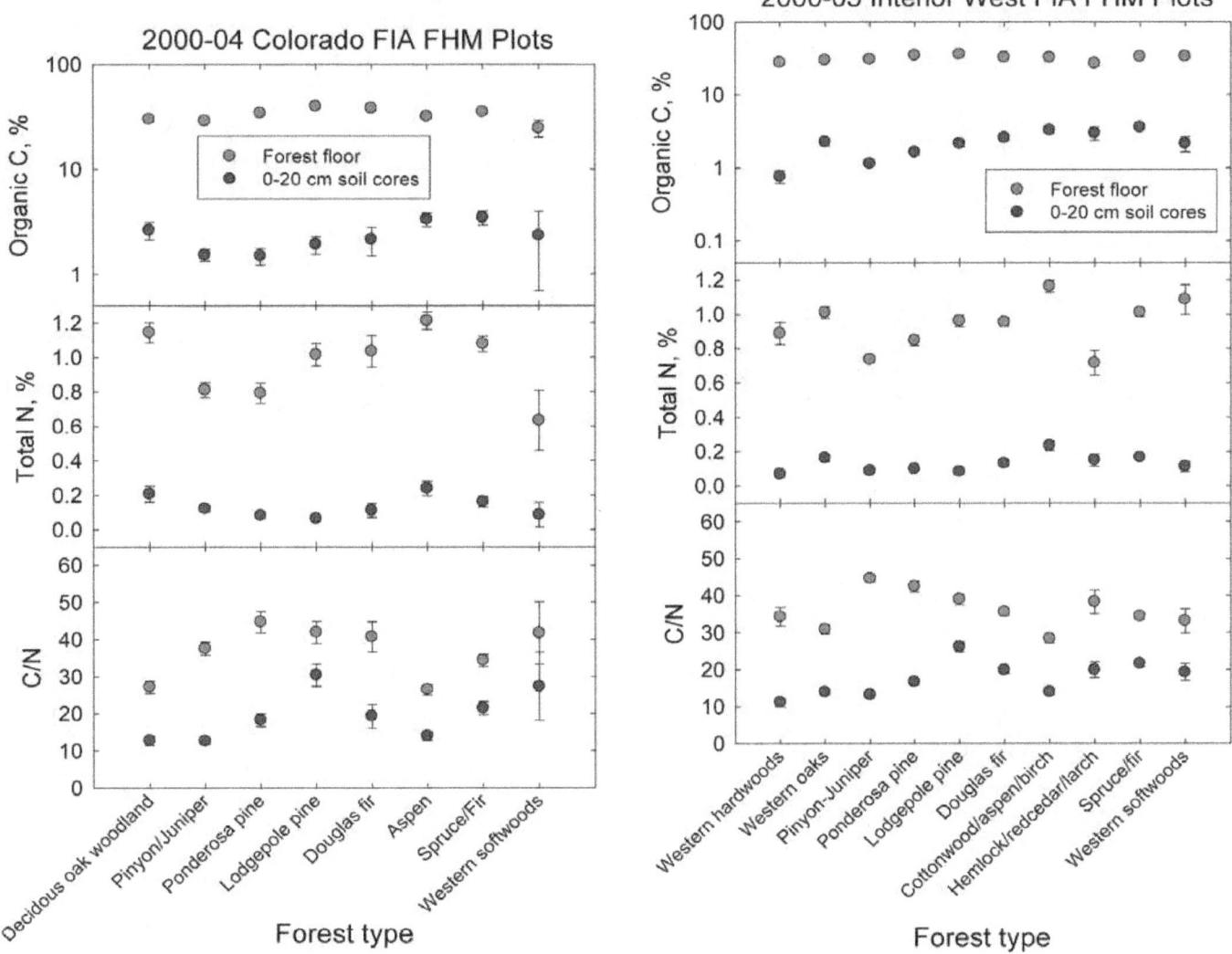

Figure 22—Forest floor and 0-20 cm mineral soil % C, % N, and C/N arranged by forest type groups in Colorado (left side) and in five Interior West States (Arizona, Colorado, Idaho, Montana, and Utah) (right side). The forest type groups are arranged left to right in order of increasing latitude, elevation, and precipitation with some overlap among forest types.

inventory (standing volume), while growth greatly exceeding removals could signal a need for increased vegetation management to decrease risks of tree mortality, insect outbreaks, or wildfire.

Removals can come from two sources: the growing-stock portion of live trees (live trees meeting specified standards of quality or vigor), or dead trees and other non-growing stock sources. The two general types of removals are timber products harvested for processing by mills and logging residue (i.e., volume cut or killed but not utilized). Removals, as reported here, are based on a 2002 survey of Colorado's primary forest products industry (Morgan and others 2006).

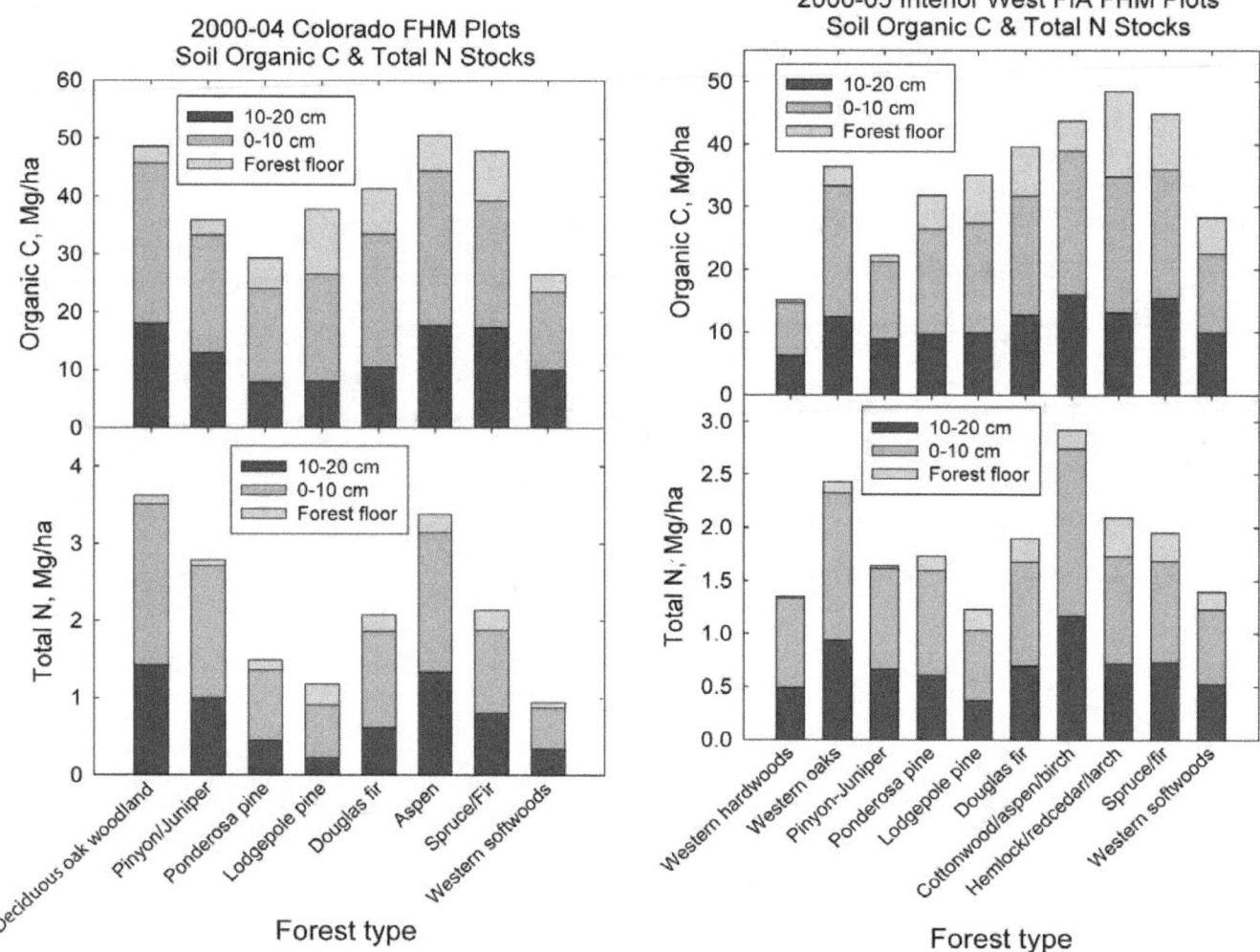

Figure 23—Soil organic carbon (top) and total nitrogen (bottom) stocks (Mg/ha) in the forest floor and 0-10 and 10-20 cm soil layers arranged by forest type groups in Colorado (left side) and in five Interior West States (Arizona, Colorado, Idaho, Montana, and Utah) (right side).

Findings

Colorado's 2002 timber harvest for industrial wood products (excluding fuelwood) was approximately 79.7 million board feet (MMBF) Scribner, about 15 million cubic feet (MMCF). Dead trees accounted for about 20 MMBF (26 percent). The 2002 harvest was 23 percent lower than the 1982 harvest (McLain 1985) and 28 percent lower than the 1999 harvest (Lynch and Mackes 2001). Timber harvest volume in Colorado is estimated to have declined by more than 5 percent since 2002. The 2007 harvest was about 75.8 MMBF Scribner, and the 2008 harvest is estimated to be lower than 2007.

Removals for total timber products (including fuelwood) totaled 34.9 MMCF during 2002 (table E4). Growing stock accounted for 11.8 MMCF (34 percent) of removals for products, with the remainder coming from other sources, including dead trees and other non-growing stock sources. Fuelwood, including residential firewood, was the leading product harvested, accounting for 54 percent of removals for products. Sawlogs accounted for 35 percent; logs chipped or shaved for composite products and excelsior accounted for 5 percent; and logs for miscellaneous products (e.g., log homes and log

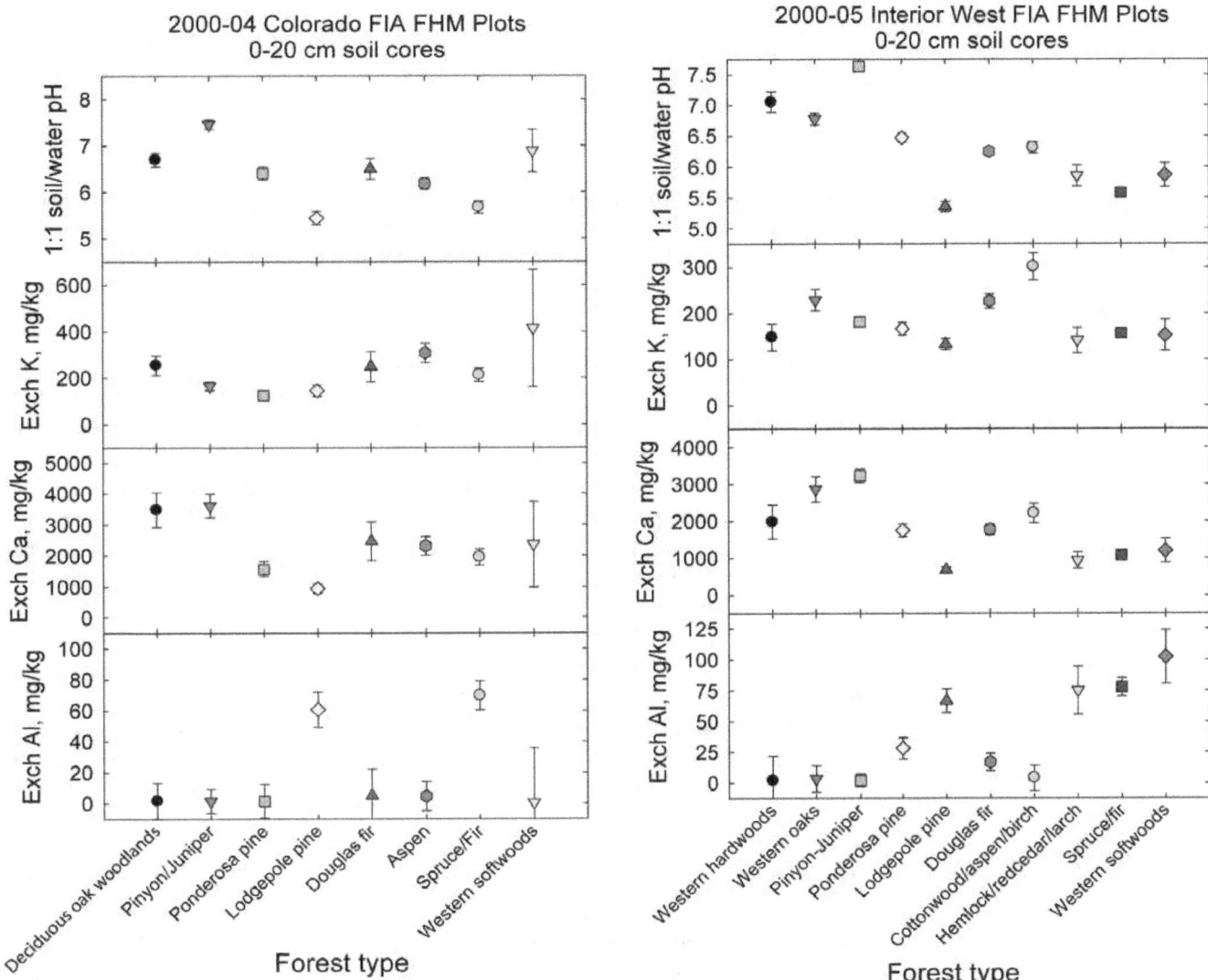

Figure 24—Soil pH and exchangeable potassium, calcium, and aluminum in the 0-20 cm soil layers arranged by forest type groups in Colorado (left side) and in five Interior West States (Arizona, Colorado, Idaho, Montana, and Utah) (right side).

furniture) accounted for 4 percent. Logs for posts, poles, and pilings accounted for the remaining 1 percent of removals for timber products. Approximately 78 percent (27.3 MMCF) of removals for products consisted of softwood species. The largest volume of hardwoods was used for fuelwood, with smaller quantities chipped or shaved for composite products/excelsior and used for sawlogs.

Total removals from Colorado's timberlands during 2002 were 38.6 MMCF (table E5). This included the 34.9 MMCF used for timber products and 3.6 MMCF of logging residue left in the forest as slash. Growing-stock removals were 12.5 MMCF. Slightly under 95 percent (11.9 MMCF) of growing-stock removals were used to produce wood products, and just over 5 percent (0.7 MMCF) were left in the forest as slash and not used. Sawlogs were the largest component (73 percent) of growing-stock removals, followed by logs chipped or shaved for composite products and excelsior (15 percent).

About 57 percent (7.1 MMCF) of growing-stock removals came from private and Tribal timberlands, while 38 percent (4.8 MMCF) came from national forests. Nearly 5 percent of the volume removed from growing stock was from other public lands.

USDA Forest Service Resour. Bull. RMRS-RB-11. 2010

39

Ponderosa pine was the leading species harvested, accounting for 25 percent (3.1 MMCF) of growing-stock removals. Aspen also represented about 25 percent, and spruce represented 23 percent. Lodgepole pine accounted for about 16 percent of growing-stock removals. Douglas-fir, true firs, and hardwoods other than aspen accounted for almost 12 percent of growing-stock removals. Ponderosa pine was the leading species harvested for most products, accounting for 39 percent of growing-stock volume harvested for products other than sawlogs and composite products. Ponderosa pine accounted for 28 percent of sawlog volume. Spruce was the leading species harvested for sawlogs. Aspen was the only species harvested for composite products and excelsior.

Interpretation

Sustainability of Colorado's forests depends on sustainable harvest levels, a forest products industry capable of utilizing harvested material, and active management of the land base available for timber production. But Colorado's annual timber harvest volume has generally been declining since the late 1980s, and the State's forest products industry has been facing mill closures and curtailments for two decades as a result of reduced harvests, particularly from Federal lands. The severe downturn in the U.S. housing market since 2005, corresponding drops in lumber prices, and the current economic recession have further exacerbated the industry's situation. However, the on-going mountain pine beetle epidemic may prove to be more challenging to forest sustainability, as the decline in Colorado's forest products industry continues to erode the ability to actively manage forests and generate income for landowners to use towards activities like hazardous fuel reduction or forest restoration, which may not generate revenue. To ensure sustainable harvest levels for future generations, careful consideration should be given not only to growth, removals, and mortality across Colorado's available timberlands, but also to the industry infrastructure that conducts management activities and uses harvested timber.

Forest Health

Forest managers, researchers, and the public have considerable concern over forest conditions in Colorado. The current mountain pine beetle epidemic in lodgepole pine forests has had a devastating visual impact in a State where recreation plays an important role in the economy. Elevated levels of mortality in spruce, fir, and pinyon pine forests have also been reported. What is the reason behind the high mortality rates? Declining forest health linked to climate change is one concern. Others speculate that several decades of fire suppression coupled with reduced levels of timber harvest on public lands have left a legacy of old, dense stands that are subject to potentially catastrophic wildfires, insect epidemics, and disease. Still others argue that periodic episodes of large-scale disturbances are expected occurrences and are natural ways for forests to regulate themselves.

How healthy or unhealthy are Colorado's forests? To answer this question, one must define 'forest health.' Forest conditions are complex and seldom permanent. Forests go through many stages as they become established, change through the growth and aging process, or are dramatically affected by a disturbance such as a mountain pine beetle epidemic. Depending on one's viewpoint, a disturbance event may be part of the natural dynamics within a healthy forest or it may be a sign that something is terribly wrong.

Colorado's forests, like many western forests, are expected to produce a sustainable mix of values such as recreation, timber production, and healthy water supplies. Most definitions of forest health contain terms relating to sustainability. Diversity, complexity, ecosystem condition, and providing for human needs are additional criteria often used to describe forest health. One traditional measure of forest sustainability is the relationship between the components of forest change (net growth, mortality, and removals) and the change in tree inventory over time. Because of the inconsistencies between the 1980s inventory and the current annual inventory, a thorough assessment of the change in tree inventory over time is not possible. The absence of a paired plot re-measurement procedure limits the analysis of forest change but it is still possible to draw assumptions from the current 'point in time' approach to estimating net growth and mortality (see "Forest Growth and Mortality" section).

The high level of conifer mortality occurring in Colorado is currently of paramount concern. The short and long term consequences of this mortality event are difficult to assess. However, examination of current mortality rates can provide a benchmark for future impacts on the inventory of live trees. Mortality rates are simply the average annual mortality estimate divided by the inventory estimate of live trees. The current annual rate of conifer mortality averages 1.2 percent. The conifer mortality rates vary by ownership (fig. 25). Conifer mortality rates on National Forest lands, where 78 percent of the conifer mortality is occurring, average over 1.3 percent annually. Mortality rates on private lands, where 9 percent of the conifer mortality is occurring, average 0.8 percent annually. Conifer mortality rates also vary by conifer species group. True firs recorded the highest annual conifer mortality rate of 2.5 percent, followed by lodgepole pine at 1.4 percent. The ponderosa and Jeffery pine species group recorded the third highest mortality rate of 1.3 percent. Annual mortality rates for the Douglas-fir, Engelmann and other spruces, and the western woodland softwood species groups average 1.0, 0.8, and 0.6 percent respectively.

What are the implications of these conifer mortality rates and what do they mean for forest health? Figure 26 illustrates the relationship between average annual mortality

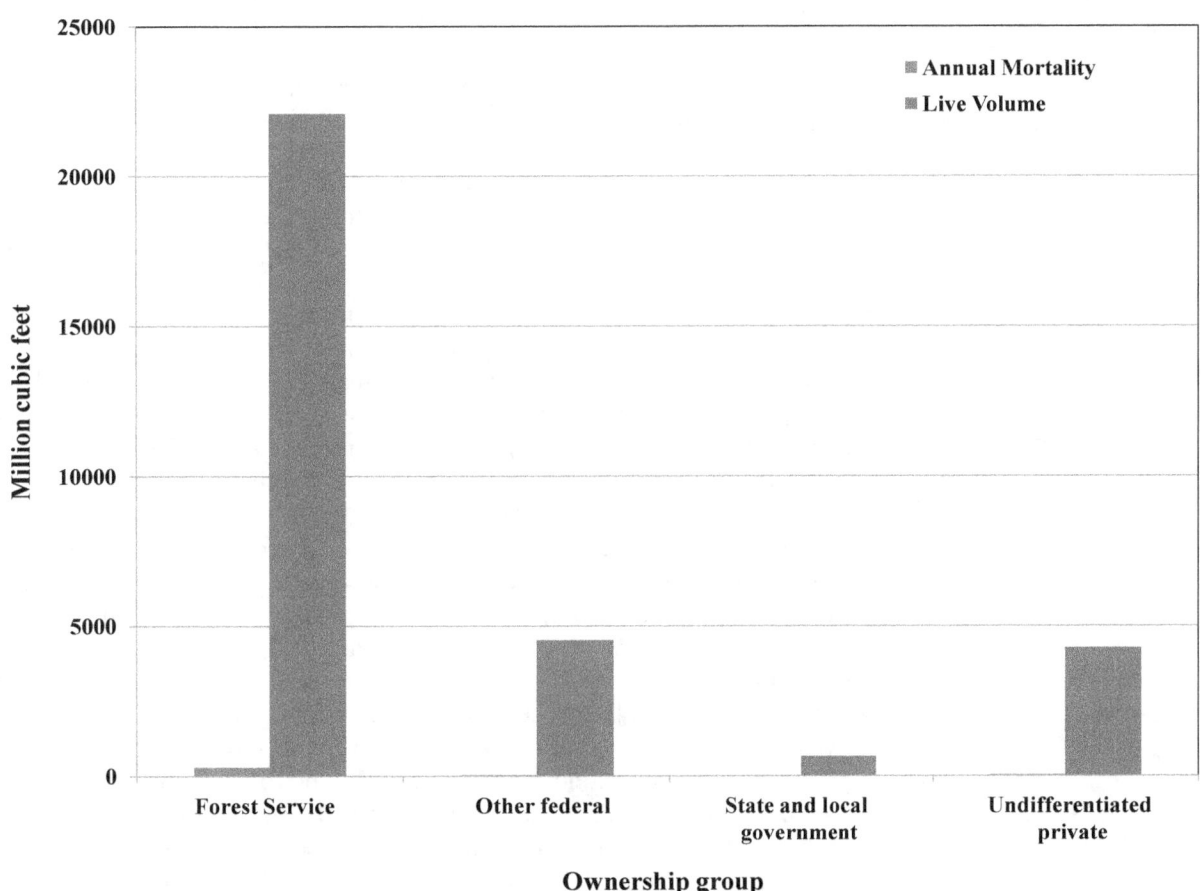

Figure 25—Volume and average annual mortality volume of live trees by ownership class, Colorado, 2002-2006.

USDA Forest Service Resour. Bull. RMRS-RB-11. 2010

41

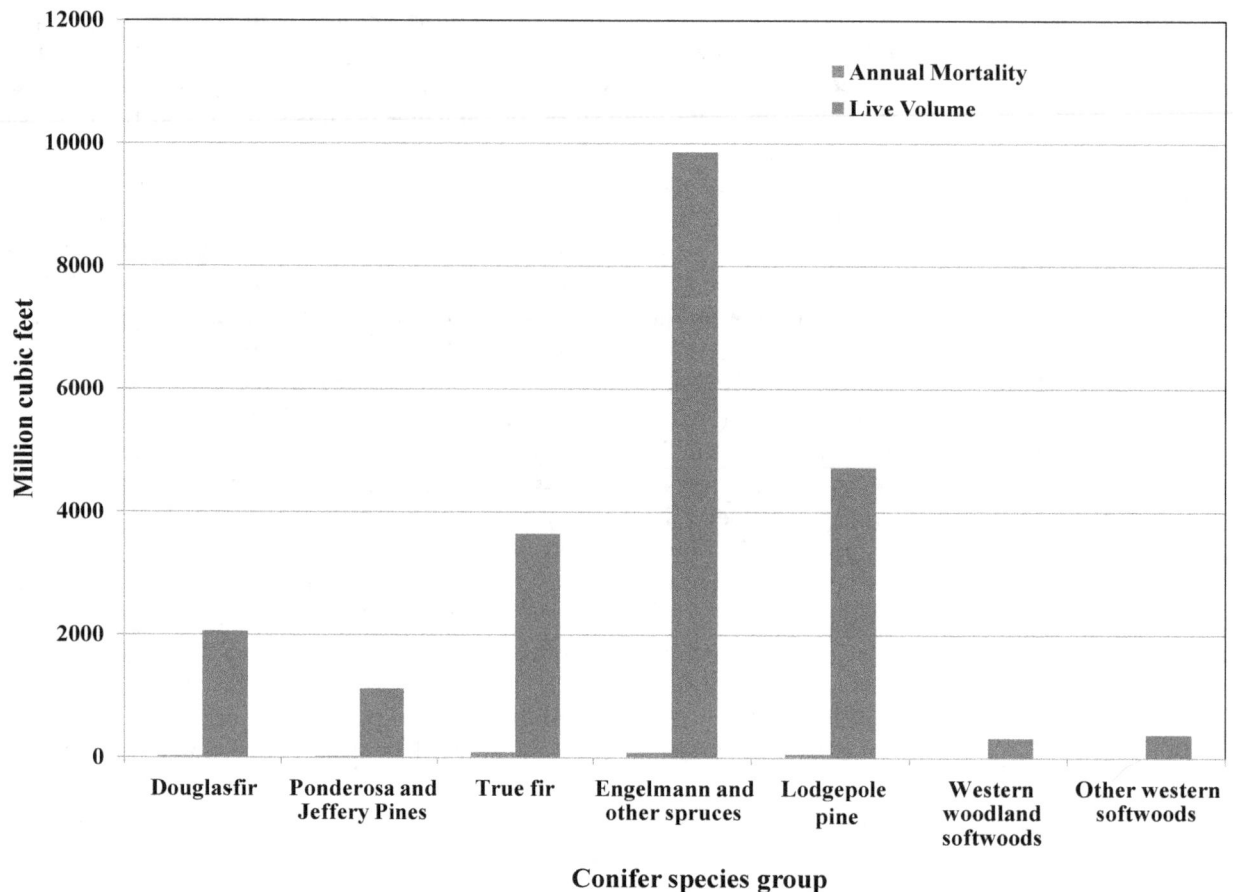

Figure 26—Volume and average annual mortality volume of live trees by species group, Colorado, 2002-2006.

and the estimate of live conifer inventory. The current conifer mortality rate will have to remain at the same level for many years or increase dramatically before the inventory of live conifers will be significantly affected. Comparing the annual conifer mortality rate of 1.2 percent to the annual conifer net annual growth rate of 0.45 percent indicates conifer inventories have been declining for several years but the decline ignores seedling and sapling size trees eventually growing into the larger diameter classes and contributing to inventory and growth estimates. Smaller trees generally have a lower susceptibility to mortality from disease and insects. Examination of the density-diameter relationship of smaller-size trees provides insight to the status of conifer regeneration. Forests with sustainable regeneration are found to have a reversed J-shaped size class distribution (West and others 1981). All of the conifer stand types in Colorado demonstrate this distribution (table 10, fig. 6). Numbers of live conifer trees in the 2-inch diameter class comprise nearly 35 percent of all live conifers. Numbers of live 2-inch trees in the true fir species group comprise 50 percent of all live true firs—the highest proportion of the major conifer species groups. In contrast, lodgepole pine registered the lowest proportion (25 percent) of trees in the smallest diameter class. However, the numbers of live lodgepole pines in the 2- and 4-inch class combined comprise 50 percent of all live lodgepole pines. The high numbers of sapling-size conifers relative to larger trees indicates sustainable conifer regeneration for the foreseeable future.

Will conifer mortality rates continue to increase? This question has generated considerable discussion with no conclusive answer. The warming of the climate and associated stresses are considered a factor in the high levels of mortality but additional research is needed into climate, natural disturbance cycles, and the mechanisms of tree mortality. Tree mortality can be a very complicated event. The exact cause of death can be difficult to determine due to the complex interaction of environmental stresses, disease, and insects. Most models of mortality are probabilities with significant variation. Should the mortality continue to increase the only thing that is certain is a reduction in average tree size. Stands affected by mortality will hold less carbon and old forest structures will decline in number. The exact impact on changes in forest composition and structure are uncertain.

Conclusions

Colorado's 23 million acres of forest land are one of the more complex ecosystems of the Interior West, with a diverse mix of coniferous and deciduous tree species. The major forest type groups in Colorado are the spruce-fir, pinyon-juniper, aspen, western oak, lodgepole pine, Douglas-fir, and ponderosa pine types. Also comprising significant areas of forest land are gambel oak, bristlecone pine, and Colorado blue spruce. The reason for this diversity is a physical landscape that ranges from flat plains and high plateaus to steep mountains and deep canyons. Within this landscape, a wide range of topographic, soil, and moisture regimes exist.

Most of Colorado's forests are controlled by public agencies. Nearly half of all forest land is controlled by National Forest Systems and 24 percent is controlled by private landowners. The significant amount of public land points to a forest resource that must meet the diverse needs of people. These needs include shelter for people and wildlife, water quality, recreation, pollution control, and timber products that furnish jobs and strengthen local economies. The population of Colorado has been growing at a tremendous rate since 1990 in many of the mountain counties (Forstall 1995). This 'mountain sprawl' has placed many homeowners in very close proximity to forest land. Naturally, people living in these settings are going to be concerned about anything that might endanger these forests and their homes, such as wildfire, insects, and disease.

The mountain pine beetle epidemic in Colorado is considered to be catastrophic and unprecedented. Forest managers have serious concerns about the future of lodgepole pine, the primary affected species. Temporal trend analysis of conifer mortality in Colorado has indicated significant increases in mortality of lodgepole pine and other conifer species through 2007 (Thompson 2009b). Whether the high level of mortality will continue into the future and what the eventual impact will be on the conifer resource in Colorado are topics for debate. The recent aspen mortality event does not appear to be reflected in the annual inventory estimates. Over time, as more years of annual data become available, aspen mortality can be evaluated with more confidence.

The information presented in this report points to opportunities for further analysis, investigation, and studies. The systematic interpenetrating panel design of the annual inventory presents opportunities to assess trends in inventory estimates never before possible with periodic inventories. Quantitative inferences about temporal trends require consideration of independent estimates of the population status each year, each of which uses completely different sample plots from different panels. Various time-series model-based estimation techniques are currently being explored (Czaplewski and Thompson 2009). These model-based estimators can not only be used to track mortality events, they can lead to better monitoring of forest growth, live tree inventory, and tree harvest activity. Once the annual inventory effort extends into the second measurement cycle in Colorado, the power to detect significant effects related to tree mortality and other parameters of interest will increase substantially with estimates derived from the re-measured (paired) plots that will be available. What is clear is the need for accurate, consistent, long-term monitoring procedures for managers and researchers to study relationships between forest attributes and changing climate patterns.

Standard Forest Inventory and Analysis Terminology _____

Average annual mortality—The average annual volume of trees 5.0 inches d.b.h./d.r.c. and larger that died from natural causes.

Average net annual growth—Average annual net change in volume of trees 5.0 inches d.b.h./d.r.c. and larger in the absence of cutting (average annual gross growth minus average annual mortality).

Basal area (BA)—The cross-sectional area of a tree stem/bole (trunk) at the point where diameter is measured, inclusive of bark. BA is calculated for trees 1.0 inch and larger in diameter, and is expressed in square feet. For timber species, the calculation is based on diameter at breast height (d.b.h.); for woodland species, it is based on diameter at root collar (d.r.c.).

Biomass—The quantity of wood fiber, for trees 1.0 inch d.b.h./d.r.c. and larger, expressed in terms of oven-dry weight. It includes above-ground portions of trees: bole/stem (trunk), bark, and branches. Biomass estimates can be computed for live and/or dead trees.

Board-foot volume—A board-foot is a unit of measure indicating the amount of wood contained in an unfinished board 1-foot wide, 1 foot long, and 1 inch thick. Board-foot volume is computed for the sawlog portion of a sawtimber-size tree; the sawlog portion includes the part of the bole on sawtimber-size tree from a 1-foot stump to a minimum sawlog top of 7 inches diameter outside bark (d.o.b.) for softwoods, or 9 inches d.o.b. for hardwoods. **Net board-foot volume** is calculated as the gross board-foot volume in the sawlog portion of a sawtimber-size tree, less deductions for cull (note: board-foot cull deductions are limited to rotten/missing material and form defect—referred to as the **merchantability factor—board-foot**). Board-foot volume estimates are computed in both Scribner and International ¼-inch rule, and can be calculated for live and/or dead (standing or down) trees.

Census water—**Streams**, sloughs, estuaries, canals, and other moving bodies of water 200 feet wide and greater, and lakes, reservoirs, ponds, and other permanent bodies of water 4.5 acres in area and greater.

Coarse woody debris—Down pieces of wood leaning more than 45 degrees from vertical with a diameter of at least 3.0 inches and a length of at least 3.0 feet.

Condition class—The combination of discrete landscape and forest attributers that identify, define, and stratify the area associated with a plot. Examples of such attributes include condition status, forest type, stand origin, stand size, owner group, and stand density.

Crown class—A classification of trees based on dominance in relation to adjacent trees in the stand as indicated by crown development and amount of sunlight received from above and the sides.

Crown cover (Canopy cover)—The percentage of the ground surface area covered by a vertical projection of plant crowns. Tree crown cover for a sample site includes the combined cover of timber and woodland trees 1.0 inch d.b.h./d.r.c. and larger. Maximum crown cover for a site is 100 percent; overlapping cover is not double counted.

Cubic-foot volume (merchantable)—A cubic-foot is a unit of measure indicating the amount of wood contained in a cube 1 by 1 by 1 foot. Cubic-foot volume is computed for the merchantable portion of timber and woodland species; the merchantable portion for timber species includes that part of a bole from a 1-foot stump to a minimum 4 inch top d.o.b, or above the place(s) of diameter measurement for any woodland tree with a single 5.0-inch stem or larger or a cumulative (calculated) d.r.c. of at least 5.0 inches to the 1.5-inch ends of all branches. **Net cubic-foot volume** is calculated as the gross cubic-foot volume in the merchantable portion of a tree, less deductions for cull.

Diameter at breast height (d.b.h.) — The diameter of a tree bole/stem (trunk) measured at breast height (4.5 feet above ground), measured outside the bark. The point of diameter measurement may vary for abnormally formed trees.

Diameter at root collar (d.r.c.) — The diameter of a tree stem(s) measured at root collar or at the point nearest the ground line (whichever is higher) that represents the basal area of the tree, measured outside the bark. For multistemmed trees, d.r.c. is calculated from an equation that incorporates the individual stem diameter measurements. The point of diameter measurement may vary for woodland trees with stems that are abnormally formed. With the exception of seedlings, woodland stems qualifying for measurement must be at least 1.0 inch in diameter or larger and at least 1.0 foot in length.

Diameter class — A grouping of tree diameters (d.b.h. or d.r.c.) into classes of a specified range. For some diameter classes, the number referenced (e.g., 4," 6," 8,") is designated as the midpoint of an individual class range. For example, if 2-inch classes are specified (the range for an individual class) and even numbers are referenced, the 6-inch class would include trees 5.0 to 6.9 inches in diameter.

Diameter outside bark (d.o.b.) — Tree diameter measurement inclusive of the outside perimeter of the tree bark. The d.o.b. measurement may be taken at various points on a tree (e.g., breast height, tree top) or log, and is sometimes estimated.

Field plot/location — A reference to the sample site or plot; an area containing the field location center (LC) and all sample points. A field location consists of four subplots and four microplots.

- **Subplot** — A 1/24-acre fixed-radius area (24-foot horizontal radius) used to sample trees 5.0 inches d.b.h./d.r.c. and larger and understory vegetation.

- **Microplot** — A 1/300-acre fixed-radius plot (6.8-foot radius), located at the center of each subplot, used to inventory seedlings and saplings.

Fixed-radius plot — A circular sample plot of a specified horizontal radius: 1/300 acre = 6.8-foot radius (microplot); 1/24 acre = 24.0-foot radius (subplot).

Forest industry land — Land owned by a company or an individual(s) operating a primary wood-processing plant.

Forest land — Land that has at least 10 percent cover of live tally tree species of any size, or land formerly having such tree cover, and not currently developed for a non-forest use. The minimum area for classification as forest land is one acre. Roadside, stream-side, and shelterbelt strips of trees must be at least 120 feet wide to qualify as forest land. Unimproved roads and trails, streams and other bodies of water, or natural clearings in forested areas are classified as forest, if less than 120 feet in width or one acre in size. Grazed woodlands, reverting fields, and pastures that are not actively maintained are included if above qualifications are satisfied.

Forest type — A classification of forest land based on the species forming a plurality of live-tree stocking.

Gross growth—The annual increase in volume of trees 5.0 inches d.b.h. and larger in absence of cutting and mortality. Gross growth includes survivor growth, ingrowth, growth on ingrowth, growth on removals before removal, and growth on mortality prior to death.

Growing-stock trees—A live timber species, 5.0 inches d.b.h. or larger, with less than 2/3 (67 percent) of the merchantable volume cull, and containing at least one solid 8-foot section, now or prospectively, reasonably free of form defect, on the merchantable portion of the tree.

Growing-stock volume—The cubic-foot volume of sound wood in growing-stock trees at least 5.0 inches d.b.h. from a 1-foot stump to a minimum 4 inch top d.o.b. to the central stem.

Hardwoods—Dicotyledonous trees, usually broadleaf and deciduous.

Hexagonal grid (Hex)—A hexagonal grid formed from equilateral triangles for the purpose of tessellating the FIA inventory sample. Each hexagon in the base grid has an area of 5,937 acres (2,403.6 ha) and contains one inventory plot. The base grid can be subdivided into smaller hexagons to intensify the sample.

Indian Trust lands—American Indian lands held in fee, or trust, by the Federal Government, but administered for tribal groups or as individual trust allotments.

Land use—The classification of a land condition by use or type.

Litter—The uppermost layer of organic debris on a forest floor; that is, essentially the freshly fallen, or only slightly decomposed material, mainly foliage, but also bark fragments, twigs, flowers, fruits, and so forth. Humus is the organic layer, unrecognizable as to origin, immediately beneath the litter layer from which it is derived. Litter and humus together are often termed duff.

Logging residue/products—

- **Bolt**—A short piece of pulpwood; a short log.

- **Industrial wood**—All commercial roundwood products, excluding fuelwood.

- **Logging residue**—The unused sections within the merchantable portions of sound (growing-stock) trees cut or killed during logging operations.

- **Mill or plant residue**—Wood material from mills or other primary manufacturing plants that is not used for the mill's or plant's primary products. Mill or plant residue includes bark, slabs, edgings, trimmings, miscuts, sawdust, and shavings. Much of the mill and plant residue is used as fuel and as the raw material for such products as pulp, palletized fuel, fiberwood, mulch, and animal bedding. Mill or plant residue includes bark and the following components:

- **Coarse residue**—Wood material suitable for chipping, such as slabs, edgings, and trim.

- **Fine residue**—Wood material unsuitable for chipping, such as sawdust and shavings.

- **Pulpwood**—Roundwood, whole-tree chips, or wood residues that are used for the production of wood pulp.

- **Roundwood**—Logs, bolts, or other round sections cut from trees.

Mapped-plot design—A sampling technique that identifies (maps) and separately classifies distinct "conditions" on the field location sample area. Each condition must meet minimum size requirements. At the most basic level, condition class delineations include forest land, nonforest land, and water. Forest land conditions can be further subdivided into separate condition classes if there are distinct variations in forest type, stand-size class, stand origin, and stand density, given that each distinct area meets minimum size requirements.

Merchantable portion—For trees measured at d.b.h. and 5.0 inches d.b.h. and larger, the merchantable portion (or "merchantable bole") includes the part of the tree bole from a 1-foot stump to a 4.0 inch top (d.o.b.). For trees measured at d.r.c., the merchantable portion includes all qualifying segments above the place(s) of diameter measurement for any tree with a single 5.0-inch stem or larger or a cumulative (calculated) d.r.c. of at least 5.0 inches to the 1.5-inch ends of all branches; sections below the place(s) of diameter measurement are not included. Qualifying segments are stems or branches that are a minimum of 1 foot in length and at least 1.0 inch in diameter; portions of stems or branches smaller than 1.0 inch in diameter, such as branch tips, are not included in the merchantable portion of the tree.

Miscellaneous Federal lands—Public lands administered by Federal agencies other than the Forest Service, U.S. Department of Agriculture, or the Bureau of Land Management, U.S. Department of the Interior.

Mortality tree—All standing or down dead trees 5.0-inches d.b.h./d.r.c. and larger that were alive within the previous 5 years.

National Forest System (NFS) lands—Public lands administered by the Forest Service, U.S. Department of Agriculture, such as National Forests, National Grasslands, and some National Recreation Areas.

National Park lands—Public lands administered by the Park Service, U.S. Department of the Interior, such as National Parks, National Monuments, National Historic Sites (such as National Memorials and National Battlefields), and some National Recreation Areas.

Noncensus water—Portions of rivers, streams, sloughs, estuaries, and canals that are 30 to 200 feet wide and at least 1 acre in size; and lakes, reservoirs, and ponds 1 to 4.5 acres in size. Portions of rivers and streams not meeting the criteria for census water, but at least 30 feet wide and 1 acre in size, are considered noncensus water. Portions of braided streams not meeting the criteria for census water, but at least 30 feet in width and 1 acre in size, and more than 50 percent water at normal high-water level are also considered noncensus water.

Nonforest land—Land that does not support, or has never supported, forests, and lands formerly forested where tree regeneration is precluded by development for other uses. Includes areas used for crops, improved pasture, residential areas, city parks, improved roads of any width and adjoining rights-of-way, power line clearings of any width, and noncensus water. If intermingled in forest areas, unimproved roads and nonforest strips must be more than 120 feet wide, and clearings, etc., more than 1 acre in size, to qualify as nonforest land.

Nonindustrial private lands—Privately owned land excluding forest industry land.

Unreserved forest land—Forest land not withdrawn from management for production of wood products through statute or administrative designation.

Other private lands—Privately owned lands other than forest industry or Indian Trust.

Other public lands—Public lands administered by agencies other than the Forest Service, U.S. Department of Agriculture. Includes lands administered by other Federal, State, county, and local government agencies, including lands leased by these agencies for more than 50 years.

Other wooded land—Land that has 5 to 10 percent cover of live tally tree species of any size, or land formerly having such tree cover, and not currently developed for a nonforest use. The minimum area for classification as forest land is one acre. Roadside, stream-side, and shelterbelt strips of trees must be at least 120 feet wide to qualify as forest land. Unimproved roads and trails, streams and other bodies of water, or natural clearings in forested areas are classified as forest, if less than 120 feet wide or one acre in size. Grazed woodlands, reverting fields, and pastures that are not actively maintained are included if above qualifications are satisfied.

Poletimber-size trees—For trees measured at d.b.h, softwoods 5.0 to 8.9 inches d.b.h. and hardwoods 5.0 to 10.9 inches d.b.h. For trees measured at d.r.c., all live trees 5.0 to 8.9 inches d.r.c.

Primary wood-processing plants—An industrial plant that processes roundwood products, such as sawlogs, pulpwood bolts, or veneer logs.

Productive forest land—Forest land capable of producing 20 cubic feet per acre per year of wood from trees classified as a timber species (see Appendix A) on forest land classified as a timber forest type (see Appendix B).

Productivity—The potential yield capability of a stand calculated as a function of site index (expressed in terms of cubic-foot growth per acre per year at age of culmination of MAI). Productivity values for forest land provide an indication of biological potential. Timberland stands are classified by the potential net annual growth attainable in fully stocked natural stands. For FIA reporting, Productivity Class is a variable that groups stand productivity values into categories of a specified range. Productivity is sometimes referred to as "Yield" or "Mean annual increment (MAI)."

Removals—The net volume of sound (growing-stock) trees removed from the inventory by harvesting or other cultural operations (such as timber-stand improvement), by land clearing, or by changes in land use (such as a shift to wilderness).

Reserved land—Land withdrawn from management for production of wood products through statute or administrative designation; examples include Wilderness areas and National Parks and Monuments.

Sampling error—A statistical term used to describe the accuracy of the inventory estimates. Expressed on a percentage basis in order to enable comparisons between the precision of different estimates, sampling errors are computed by dividing the estimate into the square root of its variance.

Sapling—A live tree 1.0-4.9 inches d.b.h./d.r.c.

Sawlog portion—The part of the bole of sawtimber-size trees between a 1-foot stump and the sawlog top.

Sawlog top—The point on the bole of sawtimber-size trees above which a sawlog cannot be produced. The minimum sawlog top is 7 inches d.o.b. for softwoods, and 9 inches d.o.b. for hardwoods.

Sawtimber-size trees—Softwoods 9.0 inches d.b.h. and larger and hardwoods 11.0 inches and larger.

Sawtimber volume—The growing-stock volume in the saw-log portion of sawtimber-size trees in board feet.

Seedlings—Live trees less than 1.0 inch d.b.h./d.r.c.

Site index—A measure of forest productivity for a timberland tree/stand. Expressed in terms of the expected height (in feet) of trees on the site at an index age of 50 (or 80 years for aspen and cottonwood). Calculated from height-to-age equations.

Site tree—A tree used to provide an index of site quality. Timber species selected for site index calculations must meet specified criteria with regards to age, diameter, crown class, and damage.

Snag—A standing-dead tree.

Softwood trees—Coniferous trees, usually evergreen, having needle- or scale-like leaves.

Stand—A community of trees that can be distinguished from adjacent communities due to similarities and uniformity in tree and site characteristics, such as age-class distribution, species composition, spatial arrangement, structure, etc.

Stand density—A relative measure that quantifies the relationship between trees per acre, stand basal area, average stand diameter, and stocking of a forested stand.

Stand density index (SDI)—A widely used measure developed by Reineke (1933), and is an index that expresses relative stand density based on a comparison of measured stand values with some standard condition; **relative stand density** is the ratio, proportion, or percent of absolute stand density to a reference level defined by some standard level of competition. For FIA reporting, the SDI for a site is usually presented as a percentage of the maximum SDI for the forest type. Site SDI values are sometimes grouped into SDI classes of a specified percentage range. Maximum SDI values vary by species and region.

Standing tree—To qualify as a standing dead tally tree, dead trees must be at least 5.0 inches in diameter, have a bole that has an unbroken actual length of at least 4.5 feet, and lean less than 45 degrees from vertical as measured from the base of the tree to 4.5 feet. Portions of boles on dead trees that are separated greater than 50 percent (either above or below 4.5 feet), are considered severed and are included in Down Woody Material (DWM) if they otherwise meet DWM tally criteria. For western woodland species with multiple stems, a tree is considered down if more than 2/3 of the volume is no longer attached or upright; do not consider cut and removed volume. For western woodland species with single stems to qualify as a standing dead tally tree, dead trees must be at least 5.0 inches in diameter, be at least 1.0 foot in unbroken actual length, and lean less than 45 degrees from vertical.

Stand-size class—A classification of forest land based on the predominant diameter size of live trees presently forming the plurality of live-tree stocking. Classes are defined as follows:

- **Sawtimber stand (Large-tree stand)**—A stand at least 10 percent stocked with live trees, in which half or more of the total stocking is from live trees 5.0 inches or larger in diameter, and with sawtimber (large tree) stocking equal to or greater than poletimber (medium tree) stocking.

- **Poletimber stand (Medium-tree stand)**—A stand at least 10 percent stocked with live trees, in which half or more of the total stocking is from live trees 5.0 inches or larger in diameter, and with poletimber (medium tree) stocking exceeding sawtimber (large tree) stocking.

- **Sapling/seedling stand**—A stand at least 10 percent stocked with live trees, in which half or more of the total stocking is from live trees less than 5.0 inches in diameter.

- **Nonstocked stand**—A formerly stocked stand that currently has less than 10 percent stocking, but has the potential to again become 10 percent stocked. For example, recently harvested, burned, or windthrow-damaged areas.

Stockability (Stockability factor)—An estimate of the stocking potential of a given site; for example, a stockability factor of 0.8 for a given site indicates that the site is capable of supporting only about 80 percent of "normal" stocking as indicated by yield tables. Stockability factors (maximum site value of 1.0) are assigned to sites based on habitat type/plant associations.

Stocking—An expression of the extent to which growing space is effectively utilized by live trees.

Timber species—Tally tree species traditionally used for industrial wood products. These include all species of conifers, except pinyon and juniper. Timber species are measured at d.b.h.

Timber stand improvement—A term comprising all intermediate cuttings or treatments, such as thinning, pruning, release cutting, girdling, weeding, or poisoning, made to improve the composition, health, and growth of the remaining trees in the stand.

Timberland—Unreserved forest land capable of producing 20 cubic feet per acre per year of wood from trees classified as a timber species (see Appendix A) on forest land designated as a timber forest type (see Appendix B).

Unproductive forest land—Forest land not capable of producing 20 cubic feet per acre per year of wood from trees classified as a timber species (see Appendix A) on forest land designated as a timber forest type and all forest lands designated as a woodland forest type (see Appendix B).

Wilderness area—An area of undeveloped land currently included in the Wilderness System, managed to preserve its natural conditions and retain its primeval character and influence.

Woodland species—Tally tree species that are not usually converted into industrial wood products. Common uses of woodland trees are fuelwood, fenceposts, and Christmas trees. These species include pinyon, juniper (except Western juniper), mesquite, locust, mountain-mahogany (*Cercocarpus* spp.), Rocky Mountain maple, bigtooth maple, desert ironwood, and most oaks (note: Bur oak and Chinkapin oak are classified as timber species). Because most woodland trees are extremely variable in form, diameter is measured at d.r.c.

Note: For the FIA national glossary please go to:

http://socrates.lv-hrc.nevada.edu/fia/ab/issues/pending/glossary.html.

References

Amman, G. D. 1973. Population changes of the mountain pine beetle in relation to elevation. Environ. Entomol. 2: 541-547.

Bailey, R.G. 1995. Descriptions of the ecoregions of the United States. (2nd ed. rev. and expanded). Misc. Publ. No. 1391. Washington, DC: U.S. Department of Agriculture, Forest Service. Online: http://csfs. colostate.edu/foresttypes.htm#ecoregions.

Bechtold, William A.; Patterson, Paul L., eds. 2005. The enhanced Forest Inventory and Analysis program—national sampling design and estimation procedures. Gen. Tech. Rep. SRS-80. Asheville, NC: U.S. Department of Agriculture, Forest Service, Southern Research Station. 85 p.

Benson, Robert E.; Green, Alan W. 1987. Colorado's timber resources. Resour. Bull. INT-48. Ogden, UT: U.S. Department of Agriculture, Forest Service, Intermountain Research Station. 53 p.

Brickell, James E 1970. Equations and computer subroutines for estimating site quality of eight Rocky Mountain Species. Res. Pap. INT-75. Ogden, UT: U.S. Department of Agriculture, Forest Service, Intermountain Research Station.

Carroll, A.L.; Safranyik, L. 2004. The bionomics of the mountain pine beetle in lodgepole pine forests: establishing a context. Pages 19-30 in T.L. Shore, J.E. Brooks, and J.E. Stone, editors. Mountain pine beetle symposium: Challenges and solutions; proceedings; October 30-31, 2003; Kelowna, British Columbia, Canada.

Chojnacky, D.C. 1985. Pinyon-juniper volume equations for the central Rocky Mountain States. Res. Note INT-339. Ogden, UT: U.S. Department of Agriculture, Forest Service, Intermountain Research Station.

Chojnacky, D.C. 1994. Volume equations for New Mexico pinyon-juniper dryland forests. Res. Note INT-471. Ogden, UT: U.S. Department of Agriculture, Forest Service, Intermountain Research Station.

Chojnacky, David C. 1984. Volume and biomass for curlleaf cercocarpus in Nevada. Res. Pap. INT-332. Ogden, UT: U.S. Department of Agriculture, Forest Service, Intermountain Forest and Range Experiment Station. 8 p.

Chojnacky, David C. 1992. Estimating volume and biomass for dryland oak species. Pages 155-161 in: Ecology and management of oak and associated woodlands: perspectives in the southwestern United States and northern Mexico; 1992 April 27-30; Sierra Vista, AZ. GTR-RM-218. Fort Collins, CO: U.S. Department of Agriculture, Forest Service, Rocky Mountain Forest and Range Experiment Station.

Chojnacky, David C.; Moisen, Gretchen. G. 1993. Converting wood volume to biomass for pinyon and juniper. Res. Note INT-411. Ogden, UT: U.S. Department of Agriculture, Forest Service, Intermountain Research Station. 5 p.

Czaplewski, R.; Thompson, M. 2009. Opportunities to improve monitoring of temporal trends with FIA panel data. Pages 1-55 in Forest Inventory and Analysis (FIA) symposium, 2008. Proc. RMRS-P-56CD, Park City, UT. Fort Collins, CO: U.S. Department of Agriculture, Forest Service, Rocky Mountain Research Station.

Edminster, C.B.; Beeson, R.T.; Metcalf, G.E. 1980. Volume tables and point-sampling factors for ponderosa pine in the Colorado Front Range. Res. Note RM-218. Fort Collins, CO: U.S. Department of Agricultue, Forest Service, Rocky Mountain Research Station.

Edminster, C.B.; Mowrer, H.T.; Hinds, T.E. 1982. Volume tables and point-sampling factors for aspen in Colorado. Res. Note RM-232. Fort Collins, CO: U.S. Department of Agriculture, Forest Service, Rocky Mountain Forest and Range Experiment Station.

Edminster, C.B.; Mowrer, H.T.; Sheppard, W.D. 1985. Site index curves for aspen in the central Rocky Mountains. Res. Note: RM-453.Fort Collins, CO: U.S. Department of Agriculture, Forest Service, Rocky Mountain Forest and Range Experiment Station 4 p.

Forstall, R. L., compiler and editor. 1995. Colorado. Population of counties by decennial census: 1900 to 1990. Washington, DC: U.S. Bureau of the Census, Population Division,. Online: http://www.census. gov/population/cencounts/co190090.txt.

Gingrich, S. F. 1967. Measuring and evaluating stocking and stand density in upland hardwood forests in the Central States. Forest Science 13:38-53.

Hann, D.W.; Bare, B.B. 1978. Comprehensive Tree volume equations for major species of NM and AZ: I. Results and methodology. Res. Note INT-209. Ogden, UT: U.S. Department of Agriculture, Forest Service, Intermountain Forest and Range Experiment Station,

Jenny, H. 1994. Factors of soil formation—a system of quantitative pedology. Dover Edition. New York: Dover Publications. 191 p.

Johnson, E. W.; Wittwer, D. 2006. Aerial detection surveys in the United States Pages 809-811 in Aguirre-Bravo, C.; Pellicane, Patrick J.; Burns, Denver P.; Draggan, Sidney, eds. Monitoring science and technology symposium: unifying knowledge for sustainability in the Western Hemisphere. Proceedings RMRS-P-42CD. Fort Collins, CO: U.S. Department of Agriculture, Forest Service, Rocky Mountain Research Station.

Kemp, P.D. 1956. Region I volume tables for ADP cruise computations. Timber Cruising Handbook, R1-2430-31. Missoula, MT: U.S. Department of Agriculture, Forest Service, Northern Region.

USDA Forest Service Resour. Bull. RMRS-RB-11. 2010

51

Lilieholm, R.J.; Long, J.N.; Patla, S. 1994. Assessing goshawk nest stand habitat using stand density index. Cooper Ornithological Society. Studies in Avian Biology 16:18-24.

Logan, J.A.; Regniere, J.; Powell, J.A. 2003 Assessing the impacts of global warming on forest pest dynamics. Frontiers in Ecology and the Environment 1: 130-137.

Long, J. N. 1985. A practical approach to density management. Forest Chronicle 61:23-37.

Long, J.N.; Daniel, T.W. 1990. Assessment of growing stock in uneven-aged stands. Western Journal of Applied Forestry 5:93-96.

Long, J.N.; Shaw, J.D. 2005. A density management diagram for even-aged ponderosa pine stands. Western Journal of Applied Forestry 20:205-215.

Lynch, D.L.; Mackes, K. 2001. Wood use in Colorado at the turn of the twenty-first century. Res. Pap. RMRS-RP-32. Fort Collins, CO: U.S. Department of Agriculture, Forest Service, Rocky Mountain Research Station. 23 p.

McLain, W.H. 1985. Colorado's industrial roundwood production and mill residue. 1982. Resour. Bull. INT-35. Ogden. UT: U.S. Department of Agriculture, Forest Service, Intermountain Research Station. 13 p.

Miller, Robert C.; Choate, Grover A. 1964. The forest resources of Colorado. Resour. Bull. Int-3. Ogden, UT: U.S. Department of Agriculture, Forest Service, Intermountain Research Station. 54 p.

Morgan, T.A.; Dillon, T.; Keegan, C.E.; Chase, A.L.; Thompson, M.T. 2006. The Four Corners timber harvest and forest products industry. 2002. Resour. Bull. RMRS-RB-7. Fort Collins, CO: U.S. Department of Agriculture, Forest Service, Rocky Mountain Research Station. 63p.

Myers, C.A. 1964. Volume table and point sampling factors for lodgepole pine in Colorado and Wyoming. Res. Note RM-6. Fort Collins, CO: U.S. Department of Agirculture, Forest Service, Rocky Mountain Forest and Range Experiment Station.

Myers, C.A.; Edminster, C.B. 1972. Volume table and point sampling factors for Engelmann spruce in Colorado and Wyoming. Res. Note RM-95. Fort Collins, CO: U.S. Department of Agriculture, Forest Service, Rocky Mountain Forest and Range Experiment Station.

Reams, G.A.; Van Deusen, P.C. 1999. The Southern Annual Forest Inventory System. Journal of Agricultural, Biological, and Environmental Statistics 4(4):346-360.

Reineke, L. H. 1933. Perfecting a stand density index for even-aged forests. Journal of Agricultural Research 46(7):627-638.

Rudinsky, J.A. 1962. Ecology of Scolytidae. Annual Review of Entomology 7: 327–348.

SAS Institute. 1999-2001. The SAS system for Windows. Release 8.02. Cary, NC: SAS Institute.

Shaw, J.D. 2000. Application of stand density index to irregularly structured stands. Western Journal of Applied Forestry 15:40-42.

Shaw, J.D.; Long, J.N. [In preparation]. Consistent definition and use of stand density index.

Shaw, John D.; Steed, Brytten E.; DeBlander, Larry T. 2005. Forest Inventory and Analysis (FIA) annual inventory answers the question: What is happening to pinyon-juniper woodlands? Journal of Forestry 103(6): 280-285.

Shinneman, D.; McClellan, R.; Smith, R. 2000. The state of the Southern Rockies Ecoregion. Nederland, CO: Southern Rockies Ecosystem Project. Online: http://csfs.colostate.edu/foresttypes.htm#ecoregions.

Smith, F.W.; Long, J.N. 1987. Elk hiding and thermal cover guidelines in the context of lodgepole pine stand density. Western Journal of Applied Forestry 2:6-10.

Stage, A.R. 1966. Simultaneous derivation of site-curve and productivity rating procedures. Society of AmerIcan Foresters Proceedings 1966:134-136. [Original equations were reformulated by J. Shaw; documentation on file at U.S. Department of Agriculture, Forest Service, Rocky Mountain Research Station, Inventory Monitoring, Ogden, UT.]

Thompson, M.T. 2009a. Mountain pine beetle infestations and sudden aspen decline in Colorado: Can the Forest Inventory and Analysis annual inventory system address the issues? In: McWilliams, Will; Moisen, Gretchen; Czaplewski, Ray, comps. Forest Inventory and Analysis (FIA) Symposium 2008; October 21-23, 2008; Park City, UT. Proc. RMRS-P-56CD. Fort Collins, CO: U.S. Department of Agriculture, Forest Service, Rocky Mountain Research Station.

Thompson, M.T. 2009b. Analysis of conifer mortality in Colorado using Forest Inventory and Analysis's annual forest inventory. Western Journal of Applied Forestry. 24(4):193-197.

U.S. Department of Agriculture, Forest Service. 1991. RMSTAND User's Guide, Chapter 60, p. 106. Unpublished user's guide on file at: U.S. Department of Agriculture, Forest Service, Southwestern Region, Albuquerque, NM.

Van Hooser, D.; Chojnacky, D.C. 1983. Whole tree volume estimates for the Rocky Mountain States. Resour. Bull. INT-29. Ogden, UT: U.S. Department of Agriculture, Forest Service, Intermountain Research Station.

West, D.C.; Shugart, H.; Ranney, J.W. 1981. Population structure of forests over a large area. Forest Science 27:701-710.

Worrall, J.J.; Egeland, L.; Eager, T.; Mask, R.A.; Johnson, E.W.; Kemp, P.A.; Shepperd, W.D. 2008. Rapid mortality of *Populus tremuloides* in southwestern Colorado, USA. Forest Ecology and Management 255: 686-696.

Appendix A: Common Name, Scientific Name, and Timber (T) or Woodland (W) Designation for Trees Measured in Colorado's Annual Inventory

Aspen (*Populus tremuloides*) T

Blue spruce (*Picea pungens*) T

Boxelder (*Acer negundo*) W

Bristlecone pine (*Pinus aristata*) W

Common or twoneedle pinyon (*Pinus edulis*) W

Curlleaf mountain-mahogany (*Cercocarpus ledifolius*) W

Douglas-fir (*Pseudotsuga menziesii*) T

Eastern cottonwood (*Populus deltoides*) T

Engelmann spruce (*Picea engelmannii*) T

Fremont cottonwood *(Populus fremontii)* T

Gambel oak (*Quercus gambelii*) W

Limber pine (*Pinus flexilis*) T

Lodgepole pine (*Pinus contorta*) T

Narrowleaf cottonwood *(Populus angustifolia)* T

Oneseed juniper (*Juniperus monosperma*) W

Plains cottonwood (*Populus sargentii*) T

Ponderosa pine (*Pinus ponderosa*) T

Rocky Mountain juniper (*Juniperus scopulorum*) W

Southwestern white pine (*Pinus strobiformus*) W

Subalpine fir (*Abies lasiocarpa*) T

Utah juniper (*Juniperus osteosperma*) W

White fir *(Abies concolor)* T

Appendix B: Forest Type Groups, Forest Type Names and Timber (T) or Woodland (W) Designation for Forest Type_____

Aspen-birch group
Aspen T

Douglas-fir group
Douglas-fir T

Elm-ash-cottonwood group
Cottonwood T

Fir-spruce-mountain hemlock group
Blue spruce T
Engelmann spruce T
Engelmann spruce-subalpine fir T
Subalpine fir T
White fir T

Lodgepole pine group
Lodgepole pine T

Nonstocked
Nonstocked (only as stand-size class) T or W

Other western hardwoods group
Cercocarpus woodland (Mountain mahogany) W
Intermountain maple woodland (Maple woodland) W

Other western softwoods group
Foxtail pine-bristlecone pine T
Limber pine T

Pinyon-juniper group
Juniper woodland W
Pinyon-juniper woodland W
Rocky Mountain juniper W

Ponderosa pine group
Ponderosa pine T

Western oak group
Deciduous oak woodland W

Appendix C: Volume, Biomass, and Site Index Equation Sources_____

Volume

Chojnacky (1985) was used for bigtooth maple, curlleaf mountain-mahogany, gamble oak, and singleleaf pinyon pine volume estimation.

Chojnacky (1994) was used for common or twoneedle pinyon pine, Rocky Mountain juniper, and Utah juniper volume estimation.

Edminster and others (1980) was used for ponderosa pine volume estimation in northeastern Utah.

Edminister and others (1982) was used for aspen volume estimation in northeastern Utah.

Hann and Bare (1978) was used for aspen, blue spruce, Douglas-fir, Engelmann spruce, Great Basin bristlecone pine, limber pine, lodgepole pine, ponderosa pine, subalpine fir, and white fir volume estimation in southwestern Utah.

Kemp (1956) was used for Fremont and narrowleaf cottonwood volume estimation.

Myers (1964) was used for limber and lodgepole pine volume estimation in northeastern Utah.

Myers and Edminister (1972) was used for blue spruce, Douglas-fir, Engelmann spruce, subalpine fir, and white fir volume estimation in northeastern Utah.

Biomass

Chojnacky (1984) was used for curlleaf mountain mahogany biomass estimation.

Chojnacky (1992) was used for bigtooth maple and gamble oak biomass estimation.

Chojnacky and Moisen (1993) was used for all juniper and pinyon species biomass estimation.

Van Hooser and Chojnacky (1983) was used for all timber (T) species biomass estimation.

Site Index

Brickell (1970) was used for blue spruce, Douglas-fir, Engelmann spruce, Great Basin bristlecone pine, limber pine, lodgepole pine, ponderosa pine, and subalpine fir site index estimation.

Edminster and others (1985) was used for aspen, and Fremont and narrowleaf cottonwood site index estimation.

Stage (1966, 1969) was used for white fir site index estimation. [Original equations were reformulated by J. Shaw; documentation on file at U.S. Department of Agriculture, Forest Service, Rocky Mountain Research Station, Inventory Monitoring, Ogden, UT.]

USDA Forest Service Resour. Bull. RMRS-RB-11. 2010

55

Appendix D: Appendix D Tables_____

Table 1—Percentage of area by land status.

Table 2—Area of accessible forest land by owner class and forest land status.

Table 3—Area of accessible forest land by forest type group and productivity class.

Table 4—Area of accessible forest land by forest type group, ownership group and land status.

Table 5—Area of accessible forest land by forest type group and stand-size class.

Table 6—Area of accessible forest land by forest type group and stand-age class.

Table 7—Area of accessible forest land by forest type group and stand origin.

Table 8—Area of forest land disturbed by forest type group and primary disturbance class.

Table 9—Area of timberland by forest type group and stand-size class.

Table 10—Number of live trees on forest land by species group and diameter class.

Table 11—Number of growing stock trees on timberland by species group and diameter class.

Table 12—Net volume of all live trees by owner class and forest land status.

Table 13—Net volume of all live trees on forest land by forest type group and stand-size class.

Table 14—Net volume of all live trees on forest land by species group and ownership group.

Table 15—Net volume of all live trees on forest land by species group and diameter class.

Table 16—Net volume of all live trees on forest land by forest type group and stand origin.

Table 17—Net volume of growing stock trees on timberland by species group and diameter class.

Table 18—Net volume of growing stock trees on timberland by species group and ownership group.

Table 19—Net volume (International $\frac{1}{4}$ inch rule) of sawtimber trees on timberland by species group and diameter class.

Table 20—Net volume of sawtimber trees on timberland by species group and ownership group.

Table 21—Average annual net growth of all live trees by owner class and forest land status.

Table 22—Average annual net growth of all live trees on forest land by forest type group and stand-size class.

Table 23—Average annual net growth of all live trees on forest land by species group and ownership group.

USDA Forest Service Resour. Bull. RMRS-RB-11. 2010

57

Table 1--Percentage of area by land status, Colorado, cycle 2, 2002-2006.

Land status	Percentage of area
Accessible forest land	
Unreserved forest land	
Timberland	16.1
Unproductive	12.0
Total unreserved forest land	28.1
Reserved forest land	
Productive	3.1
Unproductive	0.6
Total reserved forest land	3.7
All accessible forest land	31.8
Nonforest and other land	
Nonforest and other-wooded land	64.1
Water	
Census	0.3
Non-Census	0.2
All nonforest and other land	64.5
Nonsampled land	
Access denied	2.8
Hazardous conditions	0.9
Other	0.0
All land	100.0

Total area (thousands of acres)	66,620

All table cells without observations in the inventory sample are indicated by --. Table value of 0.0 indicates the percentage rounds to less than 0.1 percent. Columns and rows may not add to their totals due to rounding.

Table 2.–Area of accessible forest land by owner class and forest land status, Colorado, cycle 2, 2002-2006.

(in thousand acres)

Owner class	Unreserved forests			Reserved forests			All forest land
	Timberland	Unproductive	Total	Productive	Unproductive	Total	
Forest Service							
National Forest	7,842.2	1,228.6	9,070.8	1,962.2	68.4	2,030.7	11,101.4
National Grassland	- -	35.8	35.8	- -	- -	- -	35.8
Other Federal							
National Park Service	- -	- -	- -	176.5	162.7	339.2	339.2
Bureau of Land Management	720.0	3,867.7	4,587.7	41.7	195.2	236.9	4,824.5
Department of Defense or Energy	28.3	84.0	112.3	- -	- -	- -	112.3
State and local government							
State	305.4	348.3	653.7	- -	- -	- -	653.7
Local (county, municipal, etc.)	50.5	19.3	69.8	- -	- -	- -	69.8
Private							
Undifferentiated private	2,490.6	2,960.1	5,450.7	- -	- -	- -	5,450.7
All owners	11,437.0	8,543.8	19,980.9	2,180.4	426.4	2,606.7	22,587.6

All table cells without observations in the inventory sample are indicated by --. Table value of 0.0 indicates the acres round to less than 0.1 thousand acres. Columns and rows may not add to their totals due to rounding.

Table 3.–Area of accessible forest land by forest type group and productivity class, Colorado, cycle 2, 2002-2006.

(In thousand acres)

Forest type group	Site productivity class (cubic feet/acre/year)							All classes
	0-19	20-49	50-84	85-119	120-164	165-224	225+	
Pinyon-juniper group	5,535.6	- -	- -	- -	- -	- -	- -	5,535.6
Douglas-fir group	- -	1,563.5	190.6	- -	- -	- -	- -	1,754.1
Ponderosa pine group	- -	1,574.9	90.0	- -	- -	- -	- -	1,664.9
Fir-spruce-mountain hemlock group	24.4	2,172.8	2,101.5	377.8	- -	- -	- -	4,676.5
Lodgepole pine group	87.2	1,726.8	250.1	- -	- -	- -	- -	2,064.0
Other western softwoods group	35.0	196.7	- -	- -	- -	- -	- -	231.7
Elm-ash-cottonwood group	3.2	133.8	34.1	- -	- -	- -	- -	171.2
Aspen-birch group	242.9	1,708.5	1,067.7	65.2	26.4	- -	- -	3,110.6
Western oak group	2,573.4	- -	- -	- -	- -	- -	- -	2,573.4
Other western hardwoods group	41.4	- -	- -	- -	- -	- -	- -	41.4
Nonstocked	427.0	281.2	55.9	- -	- -	- -	- -	764.1
All forest type groups	8,970.2	9,358.3	3,789.7	443.0	26.4	- -	- -	22,587.6

All table cells without observations in the inventory sample are indicated by --. Table value of 0.0 indicates the acres round to less than 0.1 thousand acres. Columns and rows may not add to their totals due to rounding.

Table 4—Area of accessible forest land by forest type group, ownership group, and land status, Colorado, cycle 2, 2002-2006.

(In thousand acres)

Forest type group	Forest Service		Other federal		State and local government		Undifferentiated private		All forest land
	Timber-land	Other forest land	Timber-land	Other forest land	Timber-land	Other forest land	Timber-land	Other forest land	
Pinyon-juniper group	--	361.4	--	3,433.1	--	224.8	--	1,516.3	5,535.6
Douglas-fir group	875.1	94.3	244.0	--	61.8	--	478.9	--	1,754.1
Ponderosa pine group	676.3	20.4	142.2	12.5	60.5	--	753.2	--	1,664.9
Fir-spruce-mountain hemlock group	2,672.5	1,409.4	110.0	86.5	80.9	--	317.2	--	4,676.5
Lodgepole pine group	1,343.9	293.9	99.1	77.2	53.1	11.6	175.8	9.5	2,064.0
Other western softwoods group	140.2	52.7	2.7	--	--	--	36.1	--	231.7
Elm-ash-cottonwood group	2.9	--	3.3	--	21.1	--	140.6	3.2	171.2
Aspen-birch group	1,965.0	352.3	104.6	80.9	66.1	--	499.4	42.2	3,110.6
Western oak group	--	647.5	--	593.0	--	122.4	--	1,210.6	2,573.4
Other western hardwoods group	--	12.0	--	29.3	--	--	--	--	41.4
Nonstocked	166.3	51.3	42.3	215.2	12.5	8.9	89.4	178.3	764.1
All forest type groups	7,842.2	3,295.1	748.3	4,527.7	356.0	367.6	2,490.6	2,960.1	22,587.6

All table cells without observations in the inventory sample are indicated by --. Table value of 0.0 indicates the acres round to less than 0.1 thousand acres. Columns and rows may not add to their totals due to rounding.

Table 5--Area of accessible forest land by forest type group and stand-size class, Colorado, cycle 2, 2002-2006.

(In thousand acres)

Forest type group	Stand-size class					All size classes
	Large diameter	Medium diameter	Small diameter	Chaparral	Non stocked	
Pinyon-juniper group	5,147.9	131.1	256.5	--	--	5,535.6
Douglas-fir group	1,386.5	311.2	56.5	--	--	1,754.1
Ponderosa pine group	1,519.9	84.4	60.7	--	--	1,664.9
Fir-spruce-mountain hemlock group	3,558.6	761.8	356.2	--	--	4,676.5
Lodgepole pine group	996.7	875.5	191.8	--	--	2,064.0
Other western softwoods group	170.2	45.8	15.7	--	--	231.7
Elm-ash-cottonwood group	144.8	23.1	3.2	--	--	171.2
Aspen-birch group	884.4	1,715.0	511.2	--	--	3,110.6
Western oak group	41.9	139.4	2,392.2	--	--	2,573.4
Other western hardwoods group	38.3	3.0	--	--	--	41.4
Nonstocked	--	--	--	--	764.1	764.1
All forest type groups	13,889.3	4,090.2	3,844.0	--	764.1	22,587.6

All table cells without observations in the inventory sample are indicated by --. Table value of 0.0 indicates the acres round to less than 0.1 thousand acres. Columns and rows may not add to their totals due to rounding.

Table 6--Area of accessible forest land by forest type group and stand-age class, Colorado, cycle 2, 2002-2006.

(In thousand acres)

Forest type group	Non stocked	Stand-age class (years)											All classes
		1-20	21-40	41-60	61-80	81-100	101-120	121-140	141-160	161-180	181-200	201+	
Pinyon-juniper group	--	136.6	158.6	193.1	445.7	596.1	596.4	570.4	557.9	851.2	540.6	889.0	5,535.6
Douglas-fir group	--	41.7	14.8	12.5	239.9	442.0	342.2	221.5	161.6	167.0	37.6	73.5	1,754.1
Ponderosa pine group	--	50.1	27.3	34.8	247.0	536.7	544.7	145.4	155	13.6	12.3	37.5	1,664.9
Fir-spruce-mountain hemlock group	--	157.4	168.6	116.1	311.1	532.7	917.8	887.9	716.1	431.2	206.8	230.9	4,676.5
Lodgepole pine group	--	80.1	58.4	12.5	209.0	639.6	578.7	204.9	86.5	80.1	55.6	58.8	2,064.0
Other western softwoods group	--	12.5	--	--	11.2	56.0	30.5	12.5	36.8	46.6	11.9	13.6	231.7
Elm-ash-cottonwood group	--	--	13.5	12.8	69.5	38.1	26.6	4.4	--	2.9	3.3	--	171.2
Aspen-birch group	--	313.7	164.5	204.5	872.3	952.8	431.4	115.3	27.3	28.8	--	--	3,110.6
Western oak group	--	1,808.4	527.4	72.1	48.7	44.8	28.7	26.7	16.5	--	--	--	2,573.4
Other western hardwoods group	--	--	--	--	--	3.0	--	12.0	26.3	--	--	--	41.4
Nonstocked	764.1	--	--	--	--	--	--	--	--	--	--	--	764.1
All forest type groups	764.1	2,600.5	1,133.1	658.4	2,454.4	3,841.8	3,496.9	2,201.1	1,644.4	1,621.4	868.1	1,303.3	22,587.6

All table cells without observations in the inventory sample are indicated by --. Table value of 0.0 indicates the acres round to less than 0.1 thousand acres. Columns and rows may not add to their totals due to rounding.

USDA Forest Service Resour. Bull. RMRS-RB-11. 2010

61

Table 7--Area of accessible forest land by forest type group and
stand origin, Colorado, cycle 2, 2002-2006.

(In thousand acres)

| Forest type group | Stand origin | | All forest land |
	Natural stands	Artificial regeneration	
Pinyon-juniper group	5,535.6	- -	5,535.6
Douglas-fir group	1,754.1	- -	1,754.1
Ponderosa pine group	1,664.9	- -	1,664.9
Fir-spruce-mountain hemlock group	4,664.9	11.6	4,676.5
Lodgepole pine group	2,064.0	- -	2,064.0
Other western softwoods group	231.7	- -	231.7
Elm-ash-cottonwood group	171.2	- -	171.2
Aspen-birch group	3,110.6	- -	3,110.6
Western oak group	2,573.4	- -	2,573.4
Other western hardwoods group	41.4	- -	41.4
Nonstocked	764.1	- -	764.1
All forest type groups	22,576.0	11.6	22,587.6

All table cells without observations in the inventory sample are indicated by --. Table value of 0.0 indicates the
acres round to less than 0.1 thousand acres. Columns and rows may not add to their totals due to rounding.

Table 8–Area of forest land by forest type group and primary disturbance class, Colorado, cycle 2, 2002-2006.

(In thousand acres)

Forest type group	Disturbance class									All forest land
	None	Insects	Disease	Weather	Fire	Domestic animals	Wild animals	Human	Other	
Pinyon-juniper group	5,017.6	387.3	39.5	27.7	14.1	36.1	13.4	--	--	5,535.6
Douglas-fir group	1,539.5	84.1	46.6	12.8	39.7	6.5	11.4	13.5	--	1,754.1
Ponderosa pine group	1,399.8	135.0	43.2	14.2	72.7	--	--	--	--	1,664.9
Fir-spruce-mountain hemlock group	4,218.4	215.2	132.9	61.9	37.0	11.2	--	--	--	4,676.5
Lodgepole pine group	1,659.0	192.1	144.0	17.3	24.7	--	26.8	--	--	2,064.0
Other western softwoods group	207.3	21.7	--	2.7	--	--	--	--	--	231.7
Elm-ash-cottonwood group	143.8	--	8.2	--	--	19.1	--	--	--	171.2
Aspen-birch group	2,773.1	22.3	187.1	14.3	44.3	33.8	35.8	--	--	3,110.6
Western oak group	2,228.9	65.8	39.8	37.5	102.8	88.0	--	10.6	--	2,573.4
Other western hardwoods group	41.4	--	--	--	--	--	--	--	--	41.4
Nonstocked	524.7	58.6	--	15.2	156.5	9.1	--	--	--	764.1
All forest type groups	19,753.6	1,182.0	641.3	203.6	491.9	203.7	87.4	24.2	--	22,587.6

All table cells without observations in the inventory sample are indicated by --. Table value of 0.0 indicates the acres round to less than 0.1 thousand acres. Columns and rows may not add to their totals due to rounding.

Table 9–Area of timberland by forest type group and stand-size class, Colorado, cycle 2, 2002-2006.

(In thousand acres)

Forest type group	Stand-size class					All size classes
	Large diameter	Medium diameter	Small diameter	Chaparral	Non stocked	
Douglas-fir group	1,317.0	298.0	44.9	--	--	1,659.8
Ponderosa pine group	1,487.0	84.4	60.7	--	--	1,632.1
Fir-spruce-mountain hemlock group	2,353.8	591.7	235.1	--	--	3,180.6
Lodgepole pine group	751.3	755.6	164.9	--	--	1,671.9
Other western softwoods group	140.6	22.7	15.7	--	--	179.1
Elm-ash-cottonwood group	144.8	23.1	--	--	--	167.9
Aspen-birch group	840.4	1,376.5	418.3	--	--	2,635.2
Nonstocked	--	--	--	--	310.5	310.5
All forest type groups	7,034.9	3,152.0	939.6	--	310.5	11,437.0

All table cells without observations in the inventory sample are indicated by --. Table value of 0.0 indicates the acres round to less than 0.1 thousand acres. Columns and rows may not add to their totals due to rounding.

USDA Forest Service Resour. Bull. RMRS-RB-11. 2010

63

Table 10–Number of live trees on forest land by species group and diameter class, Colorado, cycle 2, 2002-2006.

(In thousand trees)

Species group	Diameter class (inches)															All classes
	1.0-2.9	3.0-4.9	5.0-6.9	7.0-8.9	9.0-10.9	11.0-12.9	13.0-14.9	15.0-16.9	17.0-18.9	19.0-20.9	21.0-24.9	25.0-28.9	29.0-32.9	33.0-36.9	37.0+	
Softwood species groups																
Western softwood species groups																
Douglas-fir	160,307	101,304	71,318	59,347	42,603	28,007	14,967	12,838	7,498	4,718	4,886	1,189	700	215	70	509,966
Ponderosa and Jeffrey pines	63,760	32,697	45,364	38,495	35,464	28,607	18,831	11,285	6,926	4,176	3,254	1,155	369	151	--	290,535
True fir	689,035	283,060	159,351	97,533	57,444	36,860	20,013	10,764	6,240	4,374	2,550	758	729	--	--	1,368,711
Engelmann and other spruces	529,939	309,451	199,978	153,267	109,762	75,547	50,964	34,309	23,306	13,066	12,206	5,260	1,003	277	--	1,518,335
Lodgepole pine	285,246	290,480	215,867	151,553	100,649	48,841	25,466	11,472	4,540	924	161	--	--	--	--	1,135,198
Western woodland softwoods	400,588	235,258	156,168	126,565	104,925	83,414	60,793	50,576	35,557	24,338	27,431	11,647	4,777	1,766	935	1,324,740
Other western softwoods	40,666	30,340	19,032	13,191	9,128	5,195	3,438	2,142	1,202	905	674	255	--	--	--	126,168
All softwoods	2,169,540	1,282,590	867,079	639,952	459,975	306,471	194,471	133,386	85,268	52,501	51,162	20,264	7,579	2,409	1,005	6,273,652
Hardwood species groups																
Western hardwood species groups																
Cottonwood and aspen	635,187	377,169	251,517	183,435	115,056	61,627	27,813	10,943	3,825	1,589	1,122	430	157	69	76	1,670,015
Other western hardwoods	1,947	974	837	226	151	452	232	154	--	--	--	--	--	--	--	4,971
Western woodland hardwoods	4,065,166	580,069	88,037	12,462	2,664	1,819	526	214	76	86	--	--	--	--	--	4,771,138
All hardwoods	4,722,301	958,232	340,390	196,123	117,870	63,898	28,570	11,310	3,825	1,665	1,208	430	157	69	76	6,446,124
All species groups	6,891,841	2,240,821	1,207,470	836,075	577,845	370,369	223,041	144,696	89,093	54,166	52,370	20,694	7,736	2,478	1,081	12,719,775

All table cells without observations in the inventory sample are indicated by --. Table value of 0 indicates the number of trees rounds to less than 1 thousand trees. Columns and rows may not add to their totals due to rounding.

Table 11--Number of growing stock trees on timberland by species group and diameter class, Colorado, cycle 2, 2002-2006.

(In thousand trees)

Species group	Diameter class (inches)													All classes
	5.0-6.9	7.0-8.9	9.0-10.9	11.0-12.9	13.0-14.9	15.0-16.9	17.0-18.9	19.0-20.9	21.0-24.9	25.0-28.9	29.0-32.9	33.0-36.9	37.0+	
Softwood species groups														
Western softwood species groups														
Douglas-fir	62,837	51,723	37,027	23,417	13,369	10,960	5,988	3,936	3,465	1,053	700	215	70	214,762
Ponderosa and Jeffrey pines	37,629	34,218	32,366	25,427	16,615	10,495	5,827	3,564	2,937	1,005	304	151	--	170,538
True fir	119,426	74,537	43,981	28,901	15,964	8,731	4,874	3,678	2,313	532	395	--	--	303,332
Engelmann and other spruces	127,480	100,664	70,630	48,919	32,423	20,862	13,705	7,661	8,054	3,303	694	196	--	434,592
Lodgepole pine	181,188	125,352	79,254	36,739	17,856	8,691	3,687	628	161	--	--	--	--	453,555
Other western softwoods	12,519	8,758	6,104	2,360	2,440	1,235	826	552	288	75	--	--	--	35,157
All softwoods	541,080	395,252	269,363	165,762	98,667	60,974	34,909	20,018	17,217	5,968	2,093	562	70	1,611,936
Hardwood species groups														
Western hardwood species groups														
Cottonwood and aspen	171,217	136,718	94,331	53,776	25,705	9,787	3,199	1,359	981	288	77	69	--	497,507
Other western hardwoods	69	--	--	75	--	75	--	--	--	--	--	--	--	220
All hardwoods	171,287	136,718	94,331	53,851	25,705	9,863	3,199	1,359	981	288	77	69	--	497,727
All species groups	712,367	531,971	363,694	219,614	124,372	70,837	38,107	21,377	18,198	6,256	2,170	632	70	2,109,663

All table cells without observations in the inventory sample are indicated by --. Table value of 0 indicates the number of trees rounds to less than 1 thousand trees. Columns and rows may not add to their totals due to rounding.

Table 12--Net volume of all live trees by owner class and forest land status, Colorado, cycle 2, 2002-2006.

(In million cubic feet)

Owner class	Unreserved forests			Reserved forests			All forest land
	Timberland	Unproductive	Total	Productive	Unproductive	Total	
Forest Service							
National Forest	19,674.1	720.2	20,394.3	5,929.0	25.0	5,954.0	26,348.3
National Grassland	- -	15.7	15.7	- -	- -	- -	15.7
Other federal							
National Park Service	- -	- -	- -	509.7	90.5	600.2	600.2
Bureau of Land Management	1,286.3	2,645.2	3,931.5	76.5	119.3	195.7	4,127.2
Department of Defense or Energy	26.2	30.9	57.1	- -	- -	- -	57.1
State and local government							
State	594.7	178.6	773.3	- -	- -	- -	773.3
Local (county, municipal, etc.)	51.0	7.3	58.2	- -	- -	- -	58.2
Private							
Undifferentiated private	4,004.0	1,279.7	5,283.8	- -	- -	- -	5,283.8
All owners	25,636.3	4,877.6	30,513.9	6,515.1	234.8	6,749.9	37,263.8

All table cells without observations in the inventory sample are indicated by --. Table value of 0.0 indicates the volume rounds to less than 0.1 million cubic feet. Columns and rows may not add to their totals due to rounding.

USDA Forest Service Resour. Bull. RMRS-RB-11. 2010

65

Table 13—Net volume of all live trees on forest land by forest type group and stand-size class, Colorado, cycle 2, 2002-2006.

(In million cubic feet)

Forest type group	Stand-size class					All size classes
	Large diameter	Medium diameter	Small diameter	Chaparral	Non stocked	
Pinyon-juniper group	4,178.0	43.6	35.7	--	--	4,257.3
Douglas-fir group	2,652.4	403.5	34.0	--	--	3,089.9
Ponderosa pine group	2,205.1	71.2	19.5	--	--	2,295.7
Fir-spruce-mountain hemlock group	13,127.7	1,521.5	112.4	--	--	14,761.7
Lodgepole pine group	3,068.7	2,112.6	115.7	--	--	5,297.1
Other western softwoods group	231.5	31.0	3.0	--	--	265.5
Elm-ash-cottonwood group	274.6	7.9	0.3	--	--	282.8
Aspen-birch group	3,083.2	3,236.1	187.8	--	--	6,507.1
Western oak group	46.7	64.9	350.1	--	--	461.7
Other western hardwoods group	11.9	0.7	--	--	--	12.5
Nonstocked	--	--	--	--	32.4	32.4
All forest type groups	28,879.9	7,493.0	858.4	--	32.4	37,263.8

All table cells without observations in the inventory sample are indicated by --. Table value of 0.0 indicates the volume rounds to less than 0.1 million cubic feet. Columns and rows may not add to their totals due to rounding.

Table 14—Net volume of all live trees on forest land by species group and ownership group, Colorado, cycle 2, 2002-2006.

(In million cubic feet)

Species group	Ownership group				All owners
	Forest Service	Other federal	State and local government	Undifferentiated private	
Softwood species groups					
Western softwood species groups					
Douglas-fir	2,055.9	418.0	80.1	743.8	3,297.9
Ponderosa and Jeffrey pines	1,117.5	156.3	107.2	1,175.7	2,556.8
True fir	3,636.5	160.2	50.5	350.2	4,197.3
Engelmann and other spruces	9,857.7	518.4	128.5	519.5	11,024.0
Lodgepole pine	4,725.0	443.0	119.2	356.7	5,643.8
Western woodland softwoods	320.9	2,783.2	151.5	1,072.9	4,328.5
Other western softwoods	376.4	42.1	1.9	37.7	458.1
All softwoods	22,090.0	4,521.2	638.8	4,256.6	31,506.5
Hardwood species groups					
Western hardwood species groups					
Cottonwood and aspen	4,206.0	240.8	191.3	936.8	5,574.9
Other western hardwoods	1.4	--	--	8.9	10.3
Western woodland hardwoods	66.6	22.5	1.5	81.4	172.0
All hardwoods	4,274.0	263.3	192.8	1,027.2	5,757.2
All species groups	26,364.0	4,784.5	831.5	5,283.8	37,263.8

All table cells without observations in the inventory sample are indicated by --. Table value of 0.0 indicates the volume rounds to less than 0.1 million cubic feet. Columns and rows may not add to their totals due to rounding.

Table 15—Net volume of all live trees on forest land by species group and diameter class, Colorado, cycle 2, 2002-2006.

(In million cubic feet)

Species group	Diameter class (Inches)													All classes
	5.0-6.9	7.0-8.9	9.0-10.9	11.0-12.9	13.0-14.9	15.0-16.9	17.0-18.9	19.0-20.9	21.0-24.9	25.0-28.9	29.0-32.9	33.0-36.9	37.0+	
Softwood species groups														
Western softwood species groups														
Douglas-fir	125	283	401	437	353	429	343	269	374	124	105	39	16	3,298
Ponderosa and Jeffrey pines	76	163	284	385	381	318	260	219	225	144	63	38	--	2,557
True fir	331	561	635	683	552	409	323	275	221	79	128	--	--	4,197
Engelmann and other spruces	428	853	1,210	1,395	1,452	1,414	1,286	927	1,158	684	161	57	--	11,024
Lodgepole pine	612	1,100	1,377	1,039	747	453	236	64	15	--	--	--	--	5,644
Western woodland softwoods	171	287	407	484	481	523	446	375	543	311	172	76	53	4,328
Other western softwoods	29	55	73	67	66	54	37	31	29	19	--	--	--	458
All softwoods	1,772	3,302	4,388	4,490	4,032	3,599	2,932	2,160	2,564	1,362	628	210	69	31,507
Hardwood species groups														
Western hardwood species groups														
Cottonwood and aspen	513	1,027	1,293	1,141	756	387	170	97	89	40	12	13	37	5,575
Other western hardwoods	1	0	1	4	2	2	--	--	--	--	--	--	--	10
Western woodland hardwoods	106	33	11	12	5	2	1	1	2	--	--	--	--	172
All hardwoods	620	1,060	1,305	1,157	764	392	170	98	91	40	12	13	37	5,757
All species groups	2,391	4,362	5,692	5,646	4,796	3,991	3,102	2,258	2,655	1,401	640	223	106	37,264

All table cells without observations in the inventory sample are indicated by --. Table value of 0 indicates the volume rounds to less than 1 million cubic feet. Columns and rows may not add to their totals due to rounding.

Table 16--Net volume of all live trees on forest land by forest type group and
stand origin, Colorado, cycle 2, 2002-2006.

(In million cubic feet)

| Forest type group | Stand origin | | All forest land |
	Natural stands	Artificial regeneration	
Pinyon-juniper group	4,257.3	- -	4,257.3
Douglas-fir group	3,089.9	- -	3,089.9
Ponderosa pine group	2,295.7	- -	2,295.7
Fir-spruce-mountain hemlock group	14,761.7	- -	14,761.7
Lodgepole pine group	5,297.1	- -	5,297.1
Other western softwoods group	265.5	- -	265.5
Elm-ash-cottonwood group	282.8	- -	282.8
Aspen-birch group	6,507.1	- -	6,507.1
Western oak group	461.7	- -	461.7
Other western hardwoods group	12.5	- -	12.5
Nonstocked	32.4	- -	32.4
All forest type groups	37,263.8	- -	37,263.8

All table cells without observations in the inventory sample are indicated by --. Table value of 0.0 indicates the
volume rounds to less than 0.1 million cubic feet. Columns and rows may not add to their totals due to rounding.

Table 17--Net volume of growing stock trees on timberland by species group and diameter class, Colorado, cycle 2, 2002-2006.

(In million cubic feet)

Species group	Diameter class (inches)													All classes
	5.0-6.9	7.0-8.9	9.0-10.9	11.0-12.9	13.0-14.9	15.0-16.9	17.0-18.9	19.0-20.9	21.0-24.9	25.0-28.9	29.0-32.9	33.0-36.9	37.0+	
Softwood species groups														
Western softwood species groups														
Douglas-fir	110	247	345	363	318	364	270	222	262	107	105	39	16	2,770
Ponderosa and Jeffrey pines	66	150	263	346	342	299	227	190	200	131	57	38	--	2,308
True fir	253	430	490	537	445	333	254	237	202	63	69	--	--	3,312
Engelmann and other spruces	285	580	803	920	951	890	780	566	769	427	113	42	--	7,125
Lodgepole pine	525	922	1,097	801	541	349	196	46	15	5	--	--	--	4,493
Other western softwoods	19	39	50	33	49	32	26	20	14	5	--	--	--	287
All softwoods	1,258	2,367	3,049	3,001	2,646	2,267	1,754	1,280	1,462	733	343	119	16	20,295
Hardwood species groups														
Western hardwood species groups														
Cottonwood and aspen	378	813	1,106	1,034	706	355	149	86	81	24	9	13	--	4,754
Other western hardwoods	0	--	--	1	--	1	--	--	--	--	--	--	--	2
All hardwoods	378	813	1,106	1,035	706	356	149	86	81	24	9	13	--	4,756
All species groups	1,636	3,180	4,155	4,036	3,352	2,623	1,903	1,366	1,543	757	352	132	16	25,051

All table cells without observations in the inventory sample are indicated by --. Table value of 0 indicates the volume rounds to less than 1 million cubic feet. Columns and rows may not add to their totals due to rounding.

Table 18–Net volume of growing stock trees on timberland by species group and ownership group, Colorado, cycle 2, 2002-2006.

(In million cubic feet)

Species group	Ownership group				All owners
	Forest Service	Other federal	State and local government	Undifferentiated private	
Softwood species groups					
Western softwood species groups					
Douglas-fir	1,639.1	352.1	68.7	709.8	2,769.7
Ponderosa and Jeffrey pines	1,025.2	125.9	99.0	1,057.8	2,307.9
True fir	2,784.9	135.2	50.3	341.7	3,312.1
Engelmann and other spruces	6,221.8	255.6	128.5	519.3	7,125.1
Lodgepole pine	3,844.7	201.9	102.3	344.5	4,493.4
Other western softwoods	229.1	18.6	1.9	37.1	286.7
All softwoods	15,744.9	1,089.3	450.6	3,010.1	20,294.9
Hardwood species groups					
Western hardwood species groups					
Cottonwood and aspen	3,558.3	174.2	186.7	834.7	4,754.0
Other western hardwoods	1.4	--	--	0.7	2.1
All hardwoods	3,559.7	174.2	186.7	835.4	4,756.1
All species groups	19,304.5	1,263.5	637.3	3,845.5	25,051.0

All table cells without observations in the inventory sample are indicated by --. Table value of 0.0 indicates the volume round to less than 0.1 million cubic feet. Columns and rows may not add to their totals due to rounding.

USDA Forest Service Resour. Bull. RMRS-RB-11. 2010

71

Table 19—Net volume of sawtimber trees (International 1/4 inch rule) on timberland by species group and diameter class, Colorado, cycle 2, 2002-2006.

(In million board feet) [1]

Species group	Diameter class (Inches)											All classes
	9.0-10.9	11.0-12.9	13.0-14.9	15.0-16.9	17.0-18.9	19.0-20.9	21.0-24.9	25.0-28.9	29.0-32.9	33.0-36.9	37.0+	
Softwood species groups												
Western softwood species groups												
Douglas-fir	1,231	1,597	1,521	1,828	1,376	1,146	1,418	598	553	234	71	11,573
Ponderosa and Jeffrey pines	814	1,390	1,544	1,443	1,150	992	1,048	725	319	200	--	9,625
True fir	1,931	2,491	2,200	1,683	1,326	1,259	1,129	354	385	--	--	12,758
Engelmann and other spruces	3,248	4,354	4,872	4,722	4,248	3,157	4,456	2,515	658	270	--	32,501
Lodgepole pine	4,060	3,479	2,570	1,721	1,025	229	85	--	--	--	--	13,171
Other western softwoods	124	111	193	140	124	94	66	26	--	--	--	879
All softwoods	11,409	13,422	12,900	11,538	9,250	6,877	8,203	4,218	1,914	704	71	80,506
Hardwood species groups												
Western hardwood species groups												
Cottonwood and aspen	--	4,586	3,348	1,721	761	442	412	94	37	51	--	11,452
Other western hardwoods	--	1	--	5	--	--	--	--	--	--	--	7
All hardwoods	--	4,588	3,348	1,727	761	442	412	94	37	51	--	11,459
All species groups	11,409	18,010	16,248	13,264	10,010	7,319	8,615	4,312	1,951	755	71	91,965

All table cells without observations in the inventory sample are indicated by --. Table value of 0 indicates the volume rounds to less than 1 million board feet. Columns and rows may not add to their totals due to rounding.
[1] International 1/4 inch rule.

72

USDA Forest Service Resour. Bull. RMRS-RB-11. 2010

Table 20—Net volume of sawtimber trees on timberland by species group and ownership group, Colorado, cycle 2, 2002-2006.

(In million cubic feet)

Species group	Ownership group				All owners
	Forest Service	Other federal	State and local government	Undifferentiated private	
Softwood species groups					
Western softwood species groups					
Douglas-fir	1,297.8	262.4	49.7	537.4	2,147.3
Ponderosa and Jeffrey pines	840.7	105.0	73.1	811.6	1,830.4
True fir	1,954.6	97.8	24.1	236.6	2,313.1
Engelmann and other spruces	4,853.4	208.0	92.7	385.1	5,539.2
Lodgepole pine	2,436.7	66.6	71.1	208.4	2,782.8
Other western softwoods	170.5	13.5	1.2	27.1	212.3
All softwoods	11,553.8	753.3	311.9	2,206.1	14,825.0
Hardwood species groups					
Western hardwood species groups					
Cottonwood and aspen	1,388.6	38.9	69.7	339.4	1,836.6
Other western hardwoods	1.1	- -	- -	0.5	1.6
All hardwoods	1,389.7	38.9	69.7	339.8	1,838.2
All species groups	12,943.5	792.2	381.6	2,545.9	16,663.2

All table cells without observations in the inventory sample are indicated by – –. Table value of 0.0 indicates the volume rounds to less than 0.1 million cubic feet. Columns and rows may not add to their totals due to rounding.

USDA Forest Service Resour. Bull. RMRS-RB-11. 2010

73

Table 21—Average annual net growth of all live trees by owner class and forest land status, Colorado, cycle 2, 2002-2006.

(In million cubic feet)

Owner class	Unreserved forests			Reserved forests			All forest land
	Timberland	Unproductive	Total	Productive	Unproductive	Total	
Forest Service							
National Forest	129.5	4.9	134.5	6.4	0.7	7.1	141.6
National Grassland	- -	0.1	0.1	- -	- -	- -	0.1
Other federal							
National Park Service	- -	- -	- -	3.2	0.6	3.8	3.8
Bureau of Land Management	3.9	9.5	13.3	1.4	0.3	1.7	15.0
Department of Defense or Energy	0.6	0.3	0.9	- -	- -	- -	0.9
State and local government							
State	9.4	-4.1	5.3	- -	- -	- -	5.3
Local (county, municipal, etc.)	0.9	0.0	0.9	- -	- -	- -	0.9
Private							
Undifferentiated private	45.3	6.9	52.2	- -	- -	- -	52.2
All owners	189.6	17.5	207.0	11.0	1.6	12.6	219.6

All table cells without observations in the inventory sample are indicated by --. Table value of 0.0 indicates the volume rounds to less than 0.1 million cubic feet. Columns and rows may not add to their totals due to rounding.

Table 22.--Average annual net growth of all live trees on forest land by forest type group and stand-size class, Colorado, cycle 2, 2002-2006.

(In million cubic feet)

| Forest type group | Stand-size class | | | | | All size classes |
	Large diameter	Medium diameter	Small diameter	Chaparral	Non stocked	
Pinyon-juniper group	15.4	0.8	-0.4	--	--	15.7
Douglas-fir group	22.3	8.3	0.2	--	--	30.7
Ponderosa pine group	20.8	1.7	0.5	--	--	23.0
Fir-spruce-mountain hemlock group	35.0	30.1	1.6	--	--	66.7
Lodgepole pine group	13.3	9.2	2.5	--	--	25.0
Other western softwoods group	2.4	0.6	0.0	--	--	3.0
Elm-ash-cottonwood group	1.0	0.3	0.0	--	--	1.3
Aspen-birch group	29.6	52.0	1.1	--	--	82.7
Western oak group	0.8	2.8	1.0	--	--	4.6
Other western hardwoods group	0.1	0.0	--	--	--	0.2
Nonstocked	--	--	--	--	-33.4	-33.4
All forest type groups	140.6	105.6	6.5	--	-33.4	219.5

All table cells without observations in the inventory sample are indicated by --. Table value of 0.0 indicates the volume rounds to less than 0.1 million cubic feet. Columns and rows may not add to their totals due to rounding.

USDA Forest Service Resour. Bull. RMRS-RB-11. 2010

75

Table 23—Average annual net growth of all live trees on forest land by species group and ownership group, Colorado, cycle 2, 2002-2006.

(In million cubic feet)

Species group	Ownership group				
	Forest Service	Other federal	State and local government	Undifferentiated private	All owners
Softwood species groups					
Western softwood species groups					
Douglas-fir	9.2	5.2	1.9	9.5	25.8
Ponderosa and Jeffrey pines	0.7	-1.6	-2.6	14.1	10.6
True fir	-8.7	-1.8	0.7	1.9	-7.9
Engelmann and other spruces	63.1	7.9	2.1	9.2	82.3
Lodgepole pine	15.2	-2.8	0.3	4.3	17.0
Western woodland softwoods	0.6	8.5	0.2	0.6	9.9
Other western softwoods	4.7	0.2	-0.2	0.6	5.3
All softwoods	84.8	15.5	2.3	40.2	142.9
Hardwood species groups					
Western hardwood species groups					
Cottonwood and aspen	54.1	3.1	3.8	8.7	69.7
Other western hardwoods	0.0	- -	- -	0.1	0.1
Western woodland hardwoods	2.7	1.0	0.0	3.2	7.0
All hardwoods	56.8	4.2	3.8	11.9	76.7
All species groups	141.6	19.6	6.2	52.2	219.6

All table cells without observations in the inventory sample are indicated by --. Table value of 0.0 indicates the volume rounds to less than 0.1 million cubic feet. Columns and rows may not add to their totals due to rounding.

Table 24—Average annual net growth of growing stock trees on timberland by species group and ownership group, Colorado, cycle 2, 2002-2006.

(In million cubic feet)

Species group	Ownership group				All owners
	Forest Service	Other federal	State and local government	Undifferentiated private	
Softwood species groups					
Western softwood species groups					
Douglas-fir	4.4	3.7	1.6	8.4	18.1
Ponderosa and Jeffrey pines	-0.7	-2.2	1.4	12.2	10.8
True fir	-1.5	-1.2	0.6	1.8	-0.3
Engelmann and other spruces	58.5	3.3	2.1	9.1	73.0
Lodgepole pine	17.1	-2.2	0.9	3.9	19.8
Western woodland softwoods	--	--	--	--	--
Other western softwoods	2.5	0.3	-0.2	0.6	3.3
All softwoods	80.4	1.8	6.4	36.1	124.6
Hardwood species groups					
Western hardwood species groups					
Cottonwood and aspen	43.2	2.1	3.7	7.2	56.2
Other western hardwoods	0.0	--	--	0.0	0.0
Western woodland hardwoods	--	--	--	--	--
All hardwoods	43.3	2.1	3.7	7.2	56.2
All species groups	123.6	3.9	10.1	43.3	180.8

All table cells without observations in the inventory sample are indicated by --. Table value of 0.0 indicates the volume rounds to less than 0.1 million cubic feet. Columns and rows may not add to their totals due to rounding.

USDA Forest Service Resour. Bull. RMRS-RB-11. 2010

77

Table 25—Average annual mortality of all live trees by owner class and forest land status, Colorado, cycle 2, 2002-2006.

(In million cubic feet)

Owner class	Unreserved forests			Reserved forests			All forest land
	Timberland	Unproductive	Total	Productive	Unproductive	Total	
Forest Service							
National Forest	236.9	8.4	245.4	80.7	0.1	80.8	326.2
National Grassland	--	--	--	--	--	--	--
Other federal							
National Park Service	--	--	--	5.5	0.2	5.7	5.7
Bureau of Land Management	22.4	11.8	34.1	0.4	0.5	0.8	35.0
Department of Defense or Energy	0.1	0.0	0.1	--	--	--	0.1
State and local government							
State	2.9	6.0	8.9	--	--	--	8.9
Local (county, municipal, etc.)	--	0.1	0.1	--	--	--	0.1
Private							
Undifferentiated private	34.1	10.9	45.0	--	--	--	45.0
All owners	296.4	37.2	333.5	86.5	0.8	87.3	420.8

All table cells without observations in the inventory sample are indicated by --. Table value of 0.0 indicates the volume rounds to less than 0.1 million cubic feet. Columns and rows may not add to their totals due to rounding.

Table 26—Average annual mortality of all live trees on forest land by forest type group and stand-size class. Colorado, cycle 2, 2002-2006.

(In million cubic feet)

Forest type group	Stand-size class					All size classes
	Large diameter	Medium diameter	Small diameter	Chaparral	Non stocked	
Pinyon-juniper group	17.3	0.2	1.2	--	--	18.6
Douglas-fir group	19.2	2.0	0.8	--	--	22.1
Ponderosa pine group	18.4	1.2	--	--	--	19.6
Fir-spruce-mountain hemlock group	167.9	9.6	2.2	--	--	179.6
Lodgepole pine group	32.1	39.0	3.4	--	--	74.4
Other western softwoods group	0.9	0.2	--	--	--	1.1
Elm-ash-cottonwood group	2.9	--	--	--	--	2.9
Aspen-birch group	26.6	26.8	4.7	--	--	58.1
Western oak group	0.1	0.1	9.7	--	--	9.8
Nonstocked	--	--	--	--	34.6	34.6
All forest type groups	285.4	79.0	21.9	--	34.6	420.8

All table cells without observations in the inventory sample are indicated by --. Table value of 0.0 indicates the volume rounds to less than 0.1 million cubic feet. Columns and rows may not add to their totals due to rounding.

USDA Forest Service Resour. Bull. RMRS-RB-11. 2010

79

Table 27—Average annual mortality of all live trees on forest land by species group and ownership group, Colorado, cycle 2, 2002-2006.

(In million cubic feet)

Species group	Ownership group				All owners
	Forest Service	Other federal	State and local government	Undifferentiated private	
Softwood species groups					
Western softwood species groups					
Douglas-fir	25.9	2.5	0.0	4.4	32.9
Ponderosa and Jeffrey pines	18.3	4.5	4.3	7.2	34.3
True fir	90.3	6.3	0.6	7.8	105.0
Engelmann and other spruces	89.1	1.0	0.4	0.8	91.3
Lodgepole pine	63.0	12.2	1.9	3.0	80.0
Western woodland softwoods	2.4	11.6	1.0	9.8	24.9
Other western softwoods	1.3	0.4	0.3	- -	2.0
All softwoods	290.4	38.5	8.5	33.0	370.3
Hardwood species groups					
Western hardwood species groups					
Cottonwood and aspen	35.7	2.1	0.4	11.5	49.7
Western woodland hardwoods	0.4	0.1	- -	0.4	0.9
All hardwoods	36.0	2.3	0.4	11.9	50.7
All species groups	326.4	40.8	8.9	44.9	421.0

All table cells without observations in the inventory sample are indicated by --. Table value of 0.0 indicates the volume rounds to less than 0.1 million cubic feet. Columns and rows may not add to their totals due to rounding.

USDA Forest Service Resour. Bull. RMRS-RB-11. 2010

Table 28—Average annual mortality of growing stock trees on timberland by species group and ownership group, Colorado, cycle 2, 2002-2006.

(In million cubic feet)

Species group	Forest Service	Other federal	Ownership group State and local government	Undifferentiated private	All owners
Softwood species groups					
Western softwood species groups					
Douglas-fir	24.7	2.5	0.0	4.4	31.7
Ponderosa and Jeffrey pines	17.4	4.5	- -	6.5	28.4
True fir	66.3	4.8	0.6	7.8	79.4
Engelmann and other spruces	45.3	0.0	0.4	0.8	46.4
Lodgepole pine	49.6	8.7	1.2	3.0	62.4
Western woodland softwoods	- -	- -	- -	- -	- -
Other western softwoods	1.2	- -	0.3	- -	1.5
All softwoods	204.4	20.5	2.5	22.5	249.8
Hardwood species groups					
Western hardwood species groups					
Cottonwood and aspen	30.1	1.6	0.4	10.7	42.8
Western woodland hardwoods	- -	- -	- -	- -	- -
All hardwoods	30.1	1.6	0.4	10.7	42.8
All species groups	234.5	22.0	2.9	33.2	292.6

All table cells without observations in the inventory sample are indicated by --. Table value of 0.0 indicates the volume rounds to less than 0.1 million cubic feet. Columns and rows may not add to their totals due to rounding.

USDA Forest Service Resour. Bull. RMRS-RB-11. 2010

81

Table 29—Aboveground dry weight of all live trees by owner class and forest land status, Colorado, cycle 2, 2002-2006.

(In thousand dry tons)

Owner class	Unreserved forests				Reserved forests				All forest land
	Timberland	Unproductive	Total		Productive	Unproductive	Total		
Forest Service									
National Forest	345,128	16,970	362,098		99,206	683	99,890		461,988
National Grassland	- -	289	289		- -	- -	- -		289
Other federal									
National Park Service	- -	- -	- -		8,769	1,985	10,754		10,754
Bureau of Land Management	24,386	51,953	76,338		1,359	2,233	3,592		79,930
Department of Defense or Energy	566	663	1,229		- -	- -	- -		1,229
State and local government									
State	10,713	3,599	14,312		- -	- -	- -		14,312
Local (county, municipal, etc.)	1,040	255	1,295		- -	- -	- -		1,295
Private									
Undifferentiated private	76,513	30,624	107,137		- -	- -	- -		107,137
All owners	458,345	104,353	562,697		109,334	4,902	114,236		676,933

All table cells without observations in the inventory sample are indicated by --. Table value of 0 indicates the aboveground tree biomass rounds to less than 1 thousand dry tons. Columns and rows may not add to their totals due to rounding.

Table 30—Aboveground dry weight of all live trees on forest land by species group and diameter class, Colorado, cycle 2, 2002-2006.

(In thousand dry tons)

Species group	Diameter class (inches)															All classes
	1.0-2.9	3.0-4.9	5.0-6.9	7.0-8.9	9.0-10.9	11.0-12.9	13.0-14.9	15.0-16.9	17.0-18.9	19.0-20.9	21.0-22.9	23.0-24.9	25.0-26.9	27.0-28.9	29.0+	
Softwood species groups																
Western softwood species groups																
Douglas-fir	882	2,482	3,264	6,167	8,128	8,530	6,735	8,001	6,296	4,945	4,796	2,029	1,263	1,016	3,053	67,587
Ponderosa and Jeffrey pines	319	654	2,153	3,253	5,330	7,237	7,296	6,190	5,173	4,337	3,258	1,224	1,600	1,192	2,044	51,260
True fir	3,771	6,086	6,767	9,480	10,012	10,354	8,111	6,127	4,825	4,230	1,920	1,409	661	781	2,083	76,619
Engelmann and other spruces	3,180	6,653	8,732	14,591	19,022	20,941	21,215	20,154	18,206	13,066	9,851	6,270	6,113	3,507	3,307	174,808
Lodgepole pine	1,426	5,810	13,018	17,763	21,407	16,393	11,917	7,084	3,642	971	226	--	--	--	--	99,658
Western woodland softwoods	771	1,868	3,458	5,358	7,336	8,621	8,543	9,350	8,189	6,842	5,429	4,443	2,966	2,609	5,387	81,169
Other western softwoods	203	607	831	1,026	1,280	1,192	1,166	935	663	605	279	276	290	61	--	9,414
All softwoods	10,551	24,160	38,223	57,639	72,515	73,268	64,983	57,841	46,994	34,996	25,759	15,652	12,893	9,166	15,874	560,514
Hardwood species groups																
Western hardwood species groups																
Cottonwood and aspen	1,270	3,583	8,797	17,287	21,788	19,455	12,879	6,702	2,955	1,601	891	581	608	--	895	99,294
Other western hardwoods	4	9	19	13	20	105	60	54	--	--	--	--	--	--	--	284
Western woodland hardwoods	5,683	5,483	3,556	1,040	342	379	170	91	--	49	47	--	--	--	--	16,840
All hardwoods	6,957	9,076	12,372	18,340	22,149	19,939	13,110	6,848	2,955	1,651	938	581	608	--	895	116,419
All species groups	17,508	33,235	50,595	75,979	94,664	93,208	78,092	64,688	49,949	36,647	26,697	16,233	13,501	9,166	16,770	676,933

All table cells without observations in the inventory sample are indicated by --. Table value of 0 indicates the aboveground tree biomass rounds to less than 1 thousand dry tons. Columns and rows may not add to their totals due to rounding.

USDA Forest Service Resour. Bull. RMRS-RB-11. 2010

83

Table 31—Area of accessible forest land by Forest Survey Unit, county and forest land status, Colorado, cycle 2, 2002-2006.

(In thousand acres)

Forest Survey Unit and county	Unreserved forests			Reserved forests			All forest land
	Timberland	Unproductive	Total	Productive	Unproductive	Total	
Northern Front Range							
Boulder	217.2	- -	217.2	16.4	- -	16.4	233.6
Clear Creek	128.8	13.6	142.4	26.1	- -	26.1	168.5
Douglas	153.3	50.6	203.9	- -	- -	- -	203.9
Elbert	15.0	- -	15.0	- -	- -	- -	15.0
El Paso	191.7	46.6	238.3	- -	- -	- -	238.3
Gilpin	84.1	9.5	93.6	- -	- -	- -	93.6
Jefferson	290.5	31.9	322.4	- -	- -	- -	322.4
Lake	97.0	13.6	110.6	19.1	- -	19.1	129.7
Larimer	647.4	50.4	697.7	182.5	- -	182.5	880.3
Park	545.2	35.0	580.2	98.5	12.5	111.1	691.3
Teller	309.2	- -	309.2	- -	- -	- -	309.2
Total	2,679.5	251.2	2,930.7	342.6	12.5	355.2	3,285.8
Southern Front Range							
Chaffee	206.6	132.9	339.6	26.1	- -	26.1	365.6
Costilla	187.3	115.7	303.1	- -	- -	- -	303.1
Custer	169.4	32.4	201.7	42.3	- -	42.3	244.1
Fremont	224.8	515.5	740.4	12.8	- -	12.8	753.1
Huerfano	135.0	266.3	401.3	54.8	- -	54.8	456.1
Las Animas	259.3	554.5	813.8	15.6	- -	15.6	829.5
Pueblo	28.7	125.8	154.5	- -	- -	- -	154.5
Total	1,211.1	1,743.2	2,954.3	151.6	- -	151.6	3,105.9
West Central							
Alamosa	- -	23.2	23.2	11.6	- -	11.6	34.7
Conejos	193.7	17.6	211.3	45.8	- -	45.8	257.1
Eagle	349.0	229.1	578.1	104.7	6.8	111.5	689.6
Grand	637.8	33.4	671.2	104.9	7.2	112.0	783.2
Gunnison	852.0	139.9	991.9	242.5	46.3	288.8	1,280.8
Hinsdale	220.2	15.3	235.5	219.8	- -	219.8	455.3
Jackson	310.5	14.4	325.0	72.2	- -	72.2	397.2
Mineral	270.1	3.0	273.1	126.8	- -	126.8	399.9
Pitkin	219.2	75.8	295.0	126.1	- -	126.1	421.0
Rio Grande	211.3	24.9	236.2	- -	- -	- -	236.2
Routt	647.7	114.1	761.8	118.2	- -	118.2	880.0
Saguache	605.7	181.9	787.6	103.5	11.9	115.4	903.0
San Juan	68.2	- -	68.2	36.7	- -	36.7	104.9
Summit	154.7	- -	154.7	70.3	- -	70.3	225.0
Total	4,740.2	872.5	5,612.7	1,383.1	72.1	1,455.3	7,067.9

(Table 31 continued on next page)

(Table 31 continued)

Forest Survey Unit and county	Unreserved forests			Reserved forests			All forest land
	Timberland	Unproductive	Total	Productive	Unproductive	Total	
Western							
Archuleta	423.4	228.5	651.9	82.5	--	82.5	734.4
Delta	131.9	193.7	325.6	--	9.8	9.8	335.4
Dolores	174.6	224.7	399.3	13.5	--	13.5	412.9
Garfield	371.6	700.4	1,072.1	134.0	--	134.0	1,206.1
La Plata	370.0	360.6	730.6	25.0	--	25.0	755.6
Mesa	356.8	866.2	1,223.0	--	61.3	61.3	1,284.3
Moffat	91.3	457.6	549.0	--	68.4	68.4	617.4
Montezuma	226.1	392.7	618.9	--	156.4	156.4	775.3
Montrose	131.8	785.6	917.4	--	31.7	31.7	949.0
Ouray	103.0	117.8	220.8	20.4	--	20.4	241.2
Rio Blanco	275.1	914.8	1,189.9	14.1	14.1	28.2	1,218.1
San Miguel	139.4	350.1	489.6	13.4	--	13.4	503.0
Total	2,795.3	5,592.8	8,388.1	303.0	341.7	644.7	9,032.8
Eastern							
Arapahoe	11.0	--	11.0	--	--	--	11.0
Baca	--	23.9	23.9	--	--	--	23.9
Bent	--	12.5	12.5	--	--	--	12.5
Otero	--	47.8	47.8	--	--	--	47.8
Total	11.0	84.2	95.1	--	--	--	95.1
All counties	11,437.0	8,543.8	19,980.9	2,180.4	426.4	2,606.7	22,587.6

All table cells without observations in the inventory sample are indicated by --. Table value of 0.0 indicates the acres round to less than 0.1 thousand acres. Columns and rows may not add to their totals due to rounding.

USDA Forest Service Resour. Bull. RMRS-RB-11. 2010

85

Table 32—Area of accessible forest land by Forest Survey Unit, county, ownership group and forest land status, Colorado, cycle 2, 2002-2006.

(In thousand acres)

Forest Survey Unit and county	Forest Service		Other federal		State and local government		Undifferentiated private		All forest land
	Timber-land	Other forest land	Timber-land	Other forest land	Timber-land	Other forest land	Timber-land	Other forest land	
Northern Front Range									
Boulder	139.4	--	--	16.4	--	--	77.9	--	233.6
Clear Creek	39.1	39.7	--	--	38.8	--	50.9	--	168.5
Douglas	128.8	--	--	--	--	2.7	24.5	48.0	203.9
Elbert	--	--	--	--	--	--	15.0	--	15.0
El Paso	87.2	--	28.3	21.8	--	23.1	76.1	1.7	238.3
Gilpin	60.1	--	--	--	12.0	--	12.0	9.5	93.6
Jefferson	91.8	--	--	--	46.5	18.1	152.2	13.8	322.4
Lake	43.4	32.7	10.9	--	--	--	42.7	--	129.7
Larimer	445.3	149.2	--	62.3	34.8	21.4	167.3	--	880.3
Park	393.9	134.8	10.4	--	8.9	--	132.0	11.2	691.3
Teller	150.1	--	12.8	--	12.8	--	133.5	--	309.2
Total	1,579.0	356.4	62.4	100.5	153.8	65.2	884.2	84.2	3,285.8
Southern Front Range									
Chaffee	182.5	58.6	3.2	56.7	--	12.7	20.9	30.9	365.6
Costilla	--	--	--	--	--	--	187.3	115.7	303.1
Custer	105.9	42.3	--	--	10.6	10.6	52.9	21.8	244.1
Fremont	47.9	44.7	99.0	343.6	28.9	42.7	49.0	97.3	753.1
Huerfano	69.2	60.6	23.1	49.9	--	--	42.7	210.7	456.1
Las Animas	15.6	15.6	--	34.0	--	60.5	243.6	460.0	829.5
Pueblo	28.7	--	--	6.1	--	28.7	--	91.0	154.5
Total	449.8	221.9	125.3	490.3	39.5	155.1	596.5	1,027.4	3,105.9

(Table 32 continued on next page)

(Table 32 continued)

Forest Survey Unit and county	Forest Service		Other federal		State and local government		Undifferentiated private		All forest land
	Timber-land	Other forest land	Timber-land	Other forest land	Timber-land	Other forest land	Timber-land	Other forest land	
West Central									
Alamosa	--	11.6	--	23.2	--	--	--	--	34.7
Conejos	171.1	45.8	12.3	--	10.3	12.3	--	5.2	257.1
Eagle	311.8	120.6	16.9	116.3	--	13.5	20.3	90.2	689.6
Grand	488.9	59.6	49.9	81.1	9.5	--	89.5	4.7	783.2
Gunnison	646.1	299.4	91.2	68.5	--	11.6	114.7	49.2	1,280.8
Hinsdale	162.9	205.0	42.0	30.1	--	--	15.3	--	455.3
Jackson	174.7	83.8	37.6	--	57.8	--	40.4	2.9	397.2
Mineral	265.7	129.8	--	--	--	--	4.4	--	399.9
Pitkin	182.8	165.5	--	24.3	--	--	36.4	12.1	421.0
Rio Grande	190.3	21.4	10.7	--	--	--	10.3	3.4	236.2
Routt	452.9	130.9	52.7	13.5	32.2	--	109.9	87.9	880.0
Saguache	530.9	198.7	36.1	74.8	3.0	--	35.7	23.8	903.0
San Juan	53.7	36.7	14.5	--	--	--	--	--	104.9
Summit	135.0	70.3	--	--	--	--	19.7	--	225.0
Total	3,766.8	1,579.1	363.9	431.7	112.8	37.4	496.6	279.6	7,067.9
Western									
Archuleta	312.8	149.5	13.7	--	--	--	96.9	161.5	734.4
Delta	113.4	9.8	--	106.9	--	9.8	18.5	77.0	335.4
Dolores	174.6	98.6	--	83.8	--	19.0	--	36.9	412.9
Garfield	183.5	159.5	117.9	520.4	--	--	70.3	154.6	1,206.1
La Plata	309.7	50.8	--	--	--	25.0	60.3	309.8	755.6
Mesa	289.7	199.0	--	643.5	--	--	67.0	85.1	1,284.3
Moffat	41.1	3.4	13.7	436.7	--	12.6	36.6	73.3	617.4
Montezuma	179.3	90.2	14.2	156.4	18.4	31.5	14.2	271.1	775.3
Montrose	78.7	225.7	--	515.6	14.1	--	39.0	76.0	949.0
Ouray	42.4	33.3	--	15.0	--	--	60.7	90.0	241.2
Rio Blanco	246.4	42.4	22.3	781.5	6.4	--	--	119.0	1,218.1
San Miguel	75.0	39.7	14.8	245.4	--	--	49.7	78.4	503.0
Total	2,046.5	1,101.8	196.6	3,505.2	38.9	97.9	513.3	1,532.6	9,032.8
Eastern									
Arapahoe	--	--	--	--	11.0	--	--	--	11.0
Baca	--	11.9	--	--	--	11.9	--	--	23.9
Bent	--	--	--	--	--	--	--	12.5	12.5
Otero	--	23.9	--	--	--	--	--	23.9	47.8
Total	--	35.8	--	--	11.0	11.9	--	36.4	95.1

(Table 32 continued)

Forest Survey Unit and county	Forest Service		Other federal		State and local government		Undifferentiated private		All forest land
	Timber-land	Other forest land	Timber-land	Other forest land	Timber-land	Other forest land	Timber-land	Other forest land	
All counties	7,842.2	3,295.1	748.3	4,527.7	356.0	367.6	2,490.6	2,960.1	22,587.6

All table cells without observations in the inventory sample are indicated by --. Table value of 0.0 indicates the acres round to less than 0.1 thousand acres. Columns and rows may not add to their totals due to rounding.

Table 33—Area of timberland by Forest Survey Unit, county and stand-size class, Colorado, cycle 2, 2002-2006.

(In thousand acres)

Forest Survey Unit and county	Stand-size class					All size classes
	Large diameter	Medium diameter	Small diameter	Chaparral	Nonstocked	
Northern Front Range						
Boulder	143.6	46.6	27.0	--	--	217.2
Clear Creek	62.8	54.3	11.7	--	--	128.8
Douglas	137.9	10.6	--	--	4.8	153.3
Elbert	12.0	--	--	--	3.0	15.0
El Paso	179.5	--	5.7	--	6.5	191.7
Gilpin	48.1	24.0	12.0	--	--	84.1
Jefferson	179.8	22.9	27.6	--	60.3	290.5
Lake	56.2	32.7	8.2	--	--	97.0
Larimer	338.4	187.2	61.5	--	60.3	647.4
Park	254.9	176.0	89.2	--	25.1	545.2
Teller	256.8	20.4	12.8	--	19.2	309.2
Total	1,669.9	574.8	255.7	--	179.1	2,679.5
Southern Front Range						
Chaffee	122.1	31.8	40.0	--	12.7	206.6
Costilla	123.5	31.5	32.3	--	--	187.3
Custer	116.4	21.2	31.8	--	--	169.4
Fremont	135.4	76.7	12.8	--	--	224.8
Huerfano	82.6	43.3	5.8	--	3.3	135.0
Las Animas	175.9	83.4	--	--	--	259.3
Pueblo	14.3	--	--	--	14.3	28.7
Total	770.3	287.8	122.6	--	30.4	1,211.1
West Central						
Conejos	145.2	36.9	11.6	--	--	193.7
Eagle	229.9	89.3	27.5	--	2.3	349.0
Grand	320.4	269.7	47.7	--	--	637.8
Gunnison	511.7	248.7	68.5	--	23.2	852.0
Hinsdale	147.6	45.9	26.7	--	--	220.2
Jackson	96.7	147.3	60.7	--	5.8	310.5
Mineral	112.7	98.3	59.1	--	--	270.1
Pitkin	102.5	80.3	36.4	--	--	219.2
Rio Grande	152.8	58.5	--	--	--	211.3
Routt	286.9	315.4	26.4	--	19.0	647.7
Saguache	282.4	221.9	86.5	--	14.9	605.7
San Juan	29.0	24.7	14.5	--	--	68.2
Summit	98.4	45.0	11.2	--	--	154.7
Total	2,516.3	1,682.0	476.8	--	65.1	4,740.2

(Table 33 continued on next page)

USDA Forest Service Resour. Bull. RMRS-RB-11. 2010

89

(Table 33 continued)

Forest Survey Unit and county	Stand-size class					All size classes
	Large diameter	Medium diameter	Small diameter	Chaparral	Nonstocked	
Western						
Archuleta	389.1	20.6	--	--	13.7	423.4
Delta	74.3	47.8	9.8	--	--	131.9
Dolores	149.1	17.4	8.1	--	--	174.6
Garfield	267.5	80.9	9.4	--	13.9	371.6
La Plata	288.7	81.3	--	--	--	370.0
Mesa	239.5	102.2	15.0	--	--	356.8
Moffat	64.0	27.4	--	--	--	91.3
Montezuma	165.8	60.4	--	--	--	226.1
Montrose	97.7	23.5	10.6	--	--	131.8
Ouray	64.4	25.8	12.9	--	--	103.0
Rio Blanco	158.5	108.4	--	--	8.2	275.1
San Miguel	108.9	11.8	18.8	--	--	139.4
Total	2,067.4	607.5	84.6	--	35.9	2,795.3
Eastern						
Arapahoe	11.0	--	--	--	--	11.0
Total	11.0	--	--	--	--	11.0
All counties	7,034.9	3,152.0	939.6	--	310.5	11,437.0

All table cells without observations in the inventory sample are indicated by --. Table value of 0.0 indicates the acres round to less than 0.1 thousand acres. Columns and rows may not add to their totals due to rounding.

USDA Forest Service Resour. Bull. RMRS-RB-11. 2010

Table 34—Area of timberland by Forest Survey Unit, county and stocking class, Colorado, cycle 2, 2002-2006.

(In thousand acres)

Forest Survey Unit and county	Stocking class of growing-stock trees					All classes
	Nonstocked	Poorly stocked	Moderately stocked	Fully stocked	Over-stocked	
Northern Front Range						
Boulder	2.5	116.3	57.3	24.7	16.4	217.2
Clear Creek	- -	23.8	74.5	13.6	17.0	128.8
Douglas	4.8	52.7	53.2	42.6	- -	153.3
Elbert	3.0	- -	12.0	- -	- -	15.0
El Paso	6.5	97.1	88.1	- -	- -	191.7
Gilpin	- -	- -	24.0	36.1	24.0	84.1
Jefferson	60.3	62.2	157.7	10.3	- -	290.5
Lake	- -	34.6	40.9	- -	21.6	97.0
Larimer	61.8	135.4	254.9	182.7	12.5	647.4
Park	25.1	169.5	194.3	153.6	2.8	545.2
Teller	28.7	152.7	115.0	12.8	- -	309.2
Total	192.8	844.2	1,071.8	476.4	94.3	2,679.5
Southern Front Range						
Chaffee	12.7	49.5	62.3	53.4	28.6	206.6
Costilla	- -	39.2	84.8	57.0	6.4	187.3
Custer	- -	34.2	95.3	18.7	21.2	169.4
Fremont	- -	71.5	102.2	51.1	- -	224.8
Huerfano	14.9	56.6	26.0	23.1	14.4	135.0
Las Animas	13.0	74.2	125.2	46.9	- -	259.3
Pueblo	14.3	14.3	- -	- -	- -	28.7
Total	54.9	339.6	495.7	250.2	70.6	1,211.1
West Central						
Conejos	- -	49.3	46.0	73.3	25.2	193.7
Eagle	15.8	44.0	121.6	128.6	39.0	349.0
Grand	- -	160.2	274.9	196.2	6.5	637.8
Gunnison	28.3	220.0	224.3	310.0	69.4	852.0
Hinsdale	- -	16.9	84.1	104.0	15.3	220.2
Jackson	5.8	40.4	161.9	102.4	- -	310.5
Mineral	- -	35.5	91.7	109.8	33.2	270.1
Pitkin	- -	49.4	48.5	84.9	36.4	219.2
Rio Grande	- -	45.6	69.3	75.1	21.4	211.3
Routt	19.0	59.6	271.0	272.3	25.8	647.7
Saguache	26.8	202.7	151.5	221.8	3.0	605.7
San Juan	- -	25.4	3.6	29.0	10.2	68.2
Summit	- -	11.2	73.1	61.9	8.4	154.7
Total	95.7	960.1	1,621.5	1,769.1	293.9	4,740.2

(Table 34 continued on next page)

USDA Forest Service Resour. Bull. RMRS-RB-11. 2010

91

(Table 34 continued)

Forest Survey Unit and county	Nonstocked	Poorly stocked	Stocking class of growing-stock trees Moderately stocked	Fully stocked	Over- stocked	All classes
Western						
Archuleta	13.7	126.7	145.6	123.7	13.7	423.4
Delta	--	38.1	19.5	54.8	19.5	131.9
Dolores	8.1	29.2	69.6	56.9	10.8	174.6
Garfield	14.2	156.7	104.1	69.0	27.7	371.6
La Plata	12.5	78.2	143.9	110.4	25.0	370.0
Mesa	--	93.8	72.6	129.0	61.4	356.8
Moffat	--	41.1	26.3	10.3	13.7	91.3
Montezuma	--	80.5	81.1	64.6	--	226.1
Montrose	--	53.1	47.0	28.2	3.5	131.8
Ouray	--	25.8	38.6	35.4	3.2	103.0
Rio Blanco	8.2	3.5	137.2	115.6	10.6	275.1
San Miguel	2.2	26.6	28.8	68.5	13.4	139.4
Total	59.0	753.1	914.2	866.3	202.7	2,795.3
Eastern						
Arapahoe	--	11.0	--	--	--	11.0
Total	--	11.0	--	--	--	11.0
All counties	402.3	2,908.0	4,103.2	3,362.1	661.4	11,437.0

All table cells without observations in the inventory sample are indicated by --. Table value of 0.0 indicates the acres round to less than 0.1 thousand acres. Columns and rows may not add to their totals due to rounding.

Table 35—Net volume of growing stock and sawtimber (International 1/4 inch rule) on timberland by Forest Survey Unit, county, and major species group, Colorado, cycle 2, 2002-2006.

Forest Survey Unit and county	Growing stock					Sawtimber				
	Major species group					Major species group				
	Pine	Other softwoods	Soft hardwoods	Hard hardwoods	All species	Pine	Other softwoods	Soft hardwoods	Hard hardwoods	All species
	(In million cubic feet)					(In million board feet)[1]				
Northern Front Range										
Boulder	170.0	129.1	0.7	--	299.8	576.2	399.5	--	--	975.7
Clear Creek	90.5	160.7	2.5	--	253.7	273.9	549.6	--	--	823.5
Douglas	110.6	132.0	13.5	--	256.1	358.0	606.3	54.6	--	1,018.9
Elbert	39.0	--	--	--	39.0	201.0	--	--	--	201.0
El Paso	136.8	84.7	0.7	--	222.2	556.8	343.4	--	--	900.3
Gilpin	83.0	125.2	2.4	--	210.5	168.8	434.1	--	--	602.9
Jefferson	194.9	125.5	12.1	--	332.5	709.9	492.5	37.4	--	1,239.9
Lake	41.1	145.7	24.2	--	211.1	83.9	561.4	--	--	645.3
Larimer	773.2	242.5	31.5	--	1,047.2	2,074.7	886.9	35.5	--	2,997.1
Park	270.0	338.7	27.7	--	636.4	869.1	1,119.8	9.6	--	1,998.6
Teller	130.5	197.0	6.8	--	334.3	488.2	819.4	5.2	--	1,312.7
Total	**2,039.5**	**1,681.1**	**122.1**	**--**	**3,842.7**	**6,360.5**	**6,212.9**	**142.4**	**--**	**12,715.8**
Southern Front Range										
Chaffee	134.4	306.6	21.5	--	462.4	436.4	1,286.8	44.7	--	1,767.9
Costilla	47.4	216.8	38.4	--	302.6	214.4	839.0	37.9	--	1,091.4
Custer	79.6	219.0	47.3	--	345.9	295.3	900.7	67.7	--	1,263.7
Fremont	75.4	243.1	10.1	--	328.6	292.7	920.5	--	--	1,213.2
Huerfano	47.0	82.1	47.9	--	177.1	144.8	306.2	129.4	--	580.4
Las Animas	154.4	142.1	68.8	--	365.3	394.6	457.4	146.6	--	998.5
Pueblo	5.3	5.3	--	--	10.6	17.8	13.1	--	--	30.9
Total	**543.4**	**1,215.0**	**234.1**	**--**	**1,992.5**	**1,795.9**	**4,723.7**	**426.4**	**--**	**6,946.0**

(Table 35 continued on next page)

(Table 35 continued)

Forest Survey Unit and county	Growing stock					Sawtimber				
	Major species group (In million cubic feet)					Major species group (In million board feet)[1]				
	Pine	Other softwoods	Soft hardwoods	Hard hardwoods	All species	Pine	Other softwoods	Soft hardwoods	Hard hardwoods	All species
West Central										
Conejos	30.8	561.4	34.8	- -	627.0	125.2	2,552.2	36.7	- -	2,714.1
Eagle	429.4	520.1	130.4	- -	1,080.0	1,675.6	2,243.5	313.8	- -	4,232.9
Grand	817.2	475.9	150.8	- -	1,443.9	2,259.0	1,898.6	287.6	- -	4,445.2
Gunnison	523.0	1,370.2	377.7	- -	2,270.9	1,574.9	6,125.3	859.2	- -	8,559.5
Hinsdale	20.2	359.0	133.9	- -	513.1	101.1	1,543.5	255.2	- -	1,899.8
Jackson	380.8	180.4	58.1	- -	619.3	922.1	695.0	112.6	- -	1,729.7
Mineral	13.5	528.4	205.5	- -	747.4	33.9	2,381.3	313.1	- -	2,728.3
Pitkin	149.7	259.9	105.1	- -	514.6	482.7	1,142.6	306.2	- -	1,931.4
Rio Grande	10.6	388.3	93.9	- -	492.7	43.3	1,558.1	254.0	- -	1,855.3
Routt	564.3	687.9	579.5	- -	1,831.7	1,902.7	2,974.0	1,160.8	- -	6,037.6
Saguache	289.9	538.8	137.1	- -	965.8	804.9	1,986.6	174.9	- -	2,966.4
San Juan	- -	137.2	33.2	- -	170.4	- -	596.2	52.5	- -	648.6
Summit	217.4	276.7	8.9	- -	503.0	637.9	1,260.1	13.7	- -	1,911.6
Total	3,446.8	6,284.1	2,048.9	- -	11,779.8	10,563.4	26,957.0	4,140.2	- -	41,660.5
Western										
Archuleta	148.5	777.0	222.6	- -	1,148.2	646.6	3,755.9	747.6	- -	5,150.0
Delta	- -	323.6	146.3	- -	469.9	- -	1,583.9	333.1	- -	1,917.0
Dolores	80.3	322.8	141.5	- -	544.5	353.3	1,547.0	526.0	- -	2,426.3
Garfield	- -	618.4	192.8	- -	811.2	- -	2,842.9	437.4	- -	3,280.3
La Plata	373.4	431.2	224.0	- -	1,028.6	1,841.9	2,171.5	606.0	- -	4,619.4
Mesa	39.2	536.0	464.7	4.8	1,044.7	186.5	2,475.8	1,265.5	18.2	3,946.0
Moffat	15.1	74.8	117.5	20.5	227.9	68.4	309.5	255.3	82.2	715.5
Montezuma	171.4	242.2	122.1	- -	535.7	790.8	1,178.8	214.7	- -	2,184.3
Montrose	29.2	83.8	147.1	- -	260.2	115.7	284.4	484.8	- -	885.0
Ouray	- -	167.9	73.2	- -	241.2	- -	815.4	209.9	- -	1,025.3
Rio Blanco	165.1	295.7	333.7	0.5	795.1	811.6	1,226.7	1,071.4	- -	3,109.7
San Miguel	35.9	153.2	132.6	- -	321.8	139.6	746.1	465.9	- -	1,351.6
Total	1,058.3	4,026.6	2,318.2	25.8	7,428.9	4,954.4	18,938.0	6,617.5	100.5	30,610.4
Eastern										
Arapahoe	- -	- -	7.0	- -	7.0	- -	- -	32.2	- -	32.2
Total	- -	- -	7.0	- -	7.0	- -	- -	32.2	- -	32.2
All counties	7,088.0	13,206.9	4,730.3	25.8	25,051.0	23,674.3	56,831.5	11,358.7	100.5	91,964.9

All table cells without observations in the inventory sample are indicated by --. Table value of 0.0 indicates the volume rounds to less than 0.1 million cubic or board feet. Columns and rows may not add to their totals due to rounding.
[1] International 1/4 inch rule.

94

USDA Forest Service Resour. Bull. RMRS-RB-11. 2010

Table 36—Average annual net growth of growing stock and sawtimber (International 1/4 inch rule) on timberland by Forest Survey Unit, county, and major species group, Colorado, cycle 2, 2002-2006.

Forest Survey Unit and county	Growing stock Major species group (In million cubic feet)					Sawtimber Major species group (In million board feet)[1]				
	Pine	Other softwoods	Soft hardwoods	Hard hardwoods	All species	Pine	Other softwoods	Soft hardwoods	Hard hardwoods	All species
Northern Front Range										
Boulder	2.3	1.6	0.1	--	3.9	11.9	11.7	--	--	23.7
Clear Creek	1.5	2.6	0.1	--	4.2	5.4	10.2	--	--	15.6
Douglas	-0.4	0.4	0.2	--	0.1	-2.4	2.8	4.3	--	4.7
Elbert	0.4	--	--	--	0.4	3.4	--	--	--	3.4
El Paso	2.3	1.9	0.1	--	4.3	12.0	9.6	-0.2	--	21.3
Gilpin	1.3	1.8	0.2	--	3.3	9.1	6.2	--	--	15.3
Jefferson	-4.9	1.3	0.3	--	-3.3	-23.7	13.6	0.7	--	-9.3
Lake	0.9	2.1	0.5	--	3.5	2.7	15.3	--	--	18.0
Larimer	13.3	-0.6	0.0	--	12.7	59.2	-3.0	-1.0	--	55.2
Park	3.0	5.2	0.2	--	8.3	16.4	27.4	-0.6	--	43.2
Teller	-3.2	2.0	-0.1	--	-1.3	-10.0	15.3	0.1	--	5.4
Total	16.4	18.3	1.4	--	36.2	84.1	109.2	3.2	--	196.6
Southern Front Range										
Chaffee	2.2	4.0	-0.7	--	5.4	9.6	14.5	1.2	--	25.3
Costilla	0.8	3.7	0.5	--	4.9	3.4	23.4	2.4	--	29.2
Custer	0.9	1.8	-0.2	--	2.4	4.2	14.7	1.1	--	19.9
Fremont	1.0	1.9	0.2	--	3.2	3.7	21.0	--	--	24.7
Huerfano	-1.7	2.0	0.5	--	0.8	-7.5	10.6	1.2	--	4.2
Las Animas	3.7	2.6	0.9	--	7.2	14.9	9.7	7.6	--	32.2
Pueblo	0.1	-3.8	0.0	--	-3.7	0.5	-18.4	--	--	-17.9
Total	7.0	12.1	1.1	--	20.2	28.8	75.4	13.4	--	117.6

(Table 36 continued on next page)

(Table 36 continued)

| Forest Survey Unit and county | Growing stock (In million cubic feet) | | | | | Sawtimber (In million board feet)[1] | | | | |
| | Major species group | | | | | Major species group | | | | |
	Pine	Other softwoods	Soft hardwoods	Hard hardwoods	All species	Pine	Other softwoods	Soft hardwoods	Hard hardwoods	All species
West Central										
Alamosa	--	--	--	--	--	--	--	--	--	--
Conejos	0.6	1.8	0.6	--	3.0	4.7	20.4	0.6	--	25.7
Eagle	6.4	-0.6	1.4	--	7.1	30.8	11.9	27.2	--	69.8
Grand	-13.5	4.4	1.4	--	-7.7	-54.1	29.1	8.6	--	-16.4
Gunnison	5.4	7.4	5.4	--	18.2	27.4	57.4	20.0	--	104.8
Hinsdale	-0.1	3.4	2.6	--	5.9	-0.1	18.6	30.4	--	48.9
Jackson	1.1	0.9	0.8	--	2.8	16.8	5.9	7.7	--	30.4
Mineral	0.5	3.1	4.7	--	8.3	2.6	16.6	19.0	--	38.1
Pitkin	2.4	-12.7	1.8	--	-8.5	14.7	-60.2	5.7	--	-39.8
Rio Grande	0.2	6.8	1.7	--	8.7	0.5	42.6	5.8	--	49.0
Routt	-0.3	6.9	4.9	--	11.6	20.4	40.0	31.8	--	92.2
Saguache	0.8	7.2	2.5	--	10.4	4.7	44.9	8.7	--	58.3
San Juan	--	1.8	0.8	--	2.6	--	7.7	0.9	--	8.6
Summit	-1.5	1.2	0.0	--	-0.3	-10.5	6.5	0.1	--	-3.9
Total	1.9	31.7	28.4	--	62.0	58.0	241.3	166.5	--	465.7
Western										
Archuleta	2.4	3.7	0.9	--	7.0	13.6	27.6	21.6	--	62.8
Delta	--	-0.7	0.8	--	0.1	--	6.0	5.6	--	11.6
Dolores	1.3	4.2	2.2	--	7.7	8.2	28.2	7.1	--	43.5
Garfield	--	3.5	2.7	--	6.1	--	28.8	37.2	--	66.0
La Plata	3.4	2.6	1.3	--	7.4	24.1	19.6	40.4	--	84.0
Mesa	0.3	5.0	6.1	0.0	11.4	1.9	29.6	32.4	0.1	64.0
Moffat	-2.5	2.4	1.2	0.5	1.6	-13.0	11.5	2.8	2.0	3.3
Montezuma	3.4	3.1	1.2	--	7.6	20.8	18.5	21.0	--	60.4
Montrose	0.8	1.2	2.0	--	3.9	5.2	2.8	21.0	--	29.0
Ouray	--	1.5	0.4	--	1.8	--	15.6	6.2	--	21.9
Rio Blanco	-1.4	1.2	5.2	-0.2	4.8	-5.9	9.0	33.7	--	36.9
San Miguel	0.7	1.1	1.0	--	2.8	2.7	5.2	18.3	--	26.1
Total	8.4	28.7	24.7	0.3	62.2	57.6	202.4	247.4	2.1	509.5
Eastern										
Arapahoe	--	--	0.3	--	0.3	--	1.5	--	--	1.5
Baca	--	--	--	--	--	--	--	--	--	--
Bent	--	--	--	--	--	--	--	--	--	--
Otero	--	--	--	--	--	--	--	--	--	--
Total	--	--	0.3	--	0.3	--	1.5	--	--	1.5

(Table 36 continued)

Forest Survey Unit and county	Growing stock					Sawtimber				
	Major species group					Major species group				
	Pine	Other softwoods	Soft hardwoods	Hard hardwoods	All species	Pine	Other softwoods	Soft hardwoods	Hard hardwoods	All species
	(In million cubic feet)					(In million board feet) [1]				
All counties	33.8	90.8	55.9	0.3	180.8	228.4	628.3	431.9	2.1	1,290.8

All table cells without observations in the inventory sample are indicated by --. Table value of 0.0 indicates the volume rounds to less than 0.1 million cubic or board feet. Columns and rows may not add to their totals due to rounding.
[1] International 1/4 inch rule.

Table 37. -- Sampling errors by Forest Survey Unit and county for area of timberland, volume, average annual net growth, average annual removals, and average annual mortality on timberland, Colorado, cycle 2, 2002-2006.

(Sampling error in percent)

Forest Survey Unit and county	Forest area	Timberland area	Growing stock				Sawtimber			
			Volume	Average annual net growth	Average annual removals	Average annual mortality	Volume	Average annual net growth	Average annual removals	Average annual mortality
Northern Front Range										
Boulder	6.47	9.13	21.26	36.66	--	51.54	25.14	23.92	--	53.88
Clear Creek	11.56	20.04	26.72	24.40	--	46.75	31.89	32.51	--	--
Douglas	8.20	17.85	25.74	100.00	--	83.55	29.52	100.00	--	90.01
Elbert	83.92	83.92	100.00	100.00	--	--	100.00	100.00	--	--
El Paso	10.70	14.95	20.27	25.92	--	94.47	21.71	22.68	--	85.31
Gilpin	2.91	15.36	27.13	35.99	--	89.57	34.87	52.35	--	100.00
Jefferson	6.83	9.28	18.28	100.00	--	41.12	19.26	100.00	--	44.12
Lake	13.67	25.06	43.25	33.84	--	100.00	58.53	62.51	--	100.00
Larimer	4.19	8.13	12.73	28.29	--	32.42	15.38	34.49	--	41.08
Park	6.33	9.10	14.11	35.08	--	51.28	14.80	30.27	--	57.46
Teller	6.21	6.21	13.10	100.00	--	58.66	13.89	100.00	--	63.16
Total	2.39	3.71	6.36	26.12	--	20.43	7.36	22.62	--	23.89
Southern Front Range										
Chaffee	8.54	17.66	29.93	36.13	--	64.25	35.76	34.05	--	59.13
Costilla	11.48	19.07	22.63	22.34	--	65.17	24.49	26.81	--	63.52
Custer	9.02	16.90	27.50	73.33	--	46.07	29.50	55.31	--	55.55
Fremont	4.37	18.92	24.78	44.35	--	42.13	26.98	30.00	--	52.00
Huerfano	8.61	26.32	35.39	100.00	--	67.74	40.44	100.00	--	76.43
Las Animas	6.66	18.17	22.45	21.00	--	50.76	24.50	28.63	--	52.56
Pueblo	20.26	64.19	97.04	100.00	--	97.04	97.04	100.00	--	97.04
Total	3.11	7.86	11.25	28.68	--	28.66	13.14	24.47	--	34.66

(Table 37 continued on next page)

(Table 37 continued)

Forest Survey Unit and county	Forest area	Timberland area	Growing stock				Sawtimber			
			Volume	Average annual net growth	Average annual removals	Average annual mortality	Volume	Average annual net growth	Average annual removals	Average annual mortality
West Central										
Alamosa	58.79	--	--	--	--	--	--	--	--	--
Conejos	11.62	17.52	25.84	100.00	--	49.06	28.82	80.80	--	54.47
Eagle	6.55	14.06	17.81	65.43	--	45.33	19.30	30.17	--	45.33
Grand	4.37	6.80	9.45	100.00	--	21.21	12.89	100.00	--	24.40
Gunnison	4.10	7.76	12.67	30.10	--	27.96	15.39	32.11	--	37.11
Hinsdale	6.14	17.89	23.23	33.22	--	34.95	24.21	53.92	--	41.41
Jackson	6.18	11.42	16.61	100.00	--	50.71	19.48	92.47	--	61.41
Mineral	5.36	13.30	22.56	38.10	--	38.59	28.29	56.43	--	45.17
Pitkin	3.31	16.35	28.25	100.00	--	86.41	33.48	100.00	--	91.40
Rio Grande	10.85	12.93	20.63	24.72	--	47.63	23.01	27.39	--	63.40
Routt	5.65	8.17	11.71	52.42	--	19.27	14.42	34.12	--	23.18
Saguache	5.54	9.52	14.44	33.00	--	45.09	15.85	31.31	--	52.35
San Juan	22.08	35.58	44.46	50.00	--	86.71	44.51	45.45	--	96.93
Summit	6.42	17.40	24.39	100.00	--	70.94	31.69	100.00	--	73.65
Total	1.77	3.23	4.92	36.77	--	14.13	6.02	25.67	--	17.36
Western										
Archuleta	3.59	12.17	17.73	94.07	--	49.49	18.67	64.86	--	55.86
Delta	8.57	24.92	33.61	100.00	--	46.79	39.72	100.00	--	56.50
Dolores	8.85	20.78	24.21	26.25	--	75.14	25.12	28.84	--	75.49
Garfield	4.74	15.43	21.31	100.00	--	72.32	23.84	63.74	--	82.08
La Plata	5.82	13.09	16.75	57.59	--	42.52	18.05	31.35	--	40.62
Mesa	4.37	16.21	20.38	24.23	--	29.06	22.56	23.12	--	33.36
Moffat	10.39	35.04	46.08	100.00	--	58.69	40.74	100.00	--	71.78
Montezuma	5.94	19.09	22.80	32.05	--	55.99	24.73	25.37	--	64.10
Montrose	4.64	28.43	35.79	39.40	--	54.04	39.22	40.12	--	80.14
Ouray	10.97	27.71	31.96	60.27	--	48.85	33.94	33.91	--	50.55
Rio Blanco	5.79	18.16	23.52	76.45	--	34.98	27.05	56.82	--	38.13
San Miguel	8.88	25.96	32.98	54.10	--	66.49	34.05	39.56	--	79.12
Total	1.82	5.42	7.06	20.93	--	16.60	7.67	15.35	--	20.18
Eastern										
Arapahoe	100.00	100.00	100.00	100.00	--	--	100.00	100.00	--	--
Baca	71.82	--	--	--	--	--	--	--	--	--
Bent	99.97	--	--	--	--	--	--	--	--	--
Otero	50.00	--	--	--	--	--	--	--	--	--
Total	35.79	100.00	100.00	100.00	--	--	100.00	100.00	--	--
All counties	1.08	2.24	3.39	15.74	--	9.38	4.00	11.79	--	11.54

Sampling errors that exceed 100% are reported as 100%. The sampling error is not calculated when the estimated value is equal to 0 and is indicated by --.

USDA Forest Service Resour. Bull. RMRS-RB-11. 2010

99

Appendix E: Appendix E Tables _____

Table E1—Maximum Stand Density Index by Forest Type.

Table E2—Mean water, carbon, and nitrogen contents of forest floor and soil cores by forest type, Colorado, 2002-2004.

Table E3a—Mean physical and chemical properties of soil cores by forest type, Colorado, 2000-2004.

Table E3b—Mean exchangeable cation concentrations in soil cores by forest type, Colorado, 2000-2004.

Table E3c—Mean extractable trace element concentrations in soil cores by forest type, Colorado, 2000-2004.

Table E4—Total roundwood output by product, species group, and source of material, Colorado, 2002.

Table E5—Volume of timber removals by source of material, species group, and removal type, Colorado, 2002.

Table E6—Quality Assurance results for condition-level variables from 81 conditions, Colorado, 2000-2006.

Table E7—Quality Assurance results for tree-level variables from 2,266 trees, Colorado, 2002-2006.

Table E1—Maximum SDI by forest type.

182 Rocky Mountain juniper	425
184 Juniper woodland	385
185 Pinyon-juniper woodland	370
201 Douglas-fir	485
221 Ponderosa pine	375
261 White fir	500
265 Engelmann spruce	500
266 ES / SAF	485
268 Subalpine fir	470
269 Colorado Blue spruce	500
281 Lodgepole pine	530
362 Southwest white pine	450
365 Foxtail / bristlecone pine	470
366 Limber pine	410
703 Cottonwood	360
706 Sugarberry / hackberry / elm / green ash	504
901 Aspen	490
925 Deciduous oak woodland	475
953 *Cercocarpus* woodland	415
999 Unknown / nonstocked	475

USDA Forest Service Resour. Bull. RMRS-RB-11. 2010

101

Table E2— Mean water, carbon, and nitrogen contents of forest floor and soil cores by forest type, Colorado, 2000-2004.

Forest type	Soil layer	Number of plots	Water content[a]	Organic carbon	Inorganic carbon	Total nitrogen	C/N ratio	Forest floor mass	Organic carbon	Total nitrogen
	cm		%	%	%	%		Mg/ha	Mg/ha	Mg/ha
Deciduous oak woodland	Forest floor	27	14.97	28.84		1.090	27.1	10.33	2.89	0.108
	0–10	18	7.39	3.12	0.34	0.247	12.6		23.62	1.825
	10–20	18	10.22	2.12	0.34	0.165	12.8		16.59	1.338
Pinyon/Juniper[b] group	Forest floor	48	8.27	26.84		0.741	37.6	9.16	2.61	0.074
	0–10	43	4.58	1.91	0.44	0.151	12.5		18.59	1.521
	10–20	33	5.43	1.19	0.51	0.093	12.7		12.41	0.960
Ponderosa pine	Forest floor	26	12.40	33.07		0.753	44.7	16.35	5.30	0.125
	0–10	22	4.32	2.13	0.20	0.122	17.4		16.61	0.928
	10–20	19	3.43	1.03	0.15	0.054	19.0		8.01	0.455
Lodgepole pine	Forest floor	22	43.54	39.28		0.959	41.9	28.53	11.24	0.272
	0–10	19	12.03	3.41	0.16	0.120	28.3		18.13	0.655
	10–20	19	7.58	1.08	0.11	0.033	33.1		7.87	0.221
Douglas fir	Forest floor	11	18.00	37.60		0.980	40.7	21.00	7.90	0.210
	0–10	9	4.37	3.75	0.17	0.198	18.8		26.62	1.389
	10–20	5	5.49	1.15	0.21	0.060	19.2		11.03	0.636
Aspen	Forest floor	36	25.39	30.15		1.150	26.5	20.08	6.18	0.239
	0–10	29	9.80	4.76	0.29	0.314	15.1		25.68	1.698
	10–20	26	7.60	2.31	0.22	0.175	13.2		17.39	1.306
Spruce/Fir group	Forest floor	45	37.13	34.10		1.034	34.3	24.83	8.56	0.261
	0–10	29	16.35	5.13	0.24	0.238	21.7		18.32	0.912
	10–20	21	11.55	2.30	0.19	0.108	21.3		15.82	0.749
Western softwoods group	Forest floor	3	9.25	24.36		0.618	41.7	10.55	2.99	0.073
	0–10	2	5.03	2.99	0.24	0.120	25.0		9.28	0.401
	10–20	2	4.92	1.90	0.15	0.065	29.6		8.25	0.297

[a]Water content and forest floor mass are reported on an oven-dry weight basis (105 °C).
[b]Pinyon/Juniper group includes Rocky Mountain juniper, juniper woodland, and pinyon/juniper woodland; Spruce/Fir group includes white fir, Engelmann spruce, subalpine fir, mixed Engelmann spruce/subalpine fir, and blue spruce; Western softwoods group includes foxtail/bristlecone pines and limber pine.

Table E3a—Mean physical and chemical properties of soil cores by forest type, Colorado, 2000-2004.

Forest type	Soil layer	Number of plots	SQI[a]	Bulk density	Coarse fragments	pH H₂O	pH CaCl₂	Bray 1 extractable phosphorus	Olsen extractable phosphorus
	cm		%	g/cm³	%			mg/kg	mg/kg
Deciduous oak woodland	0–10	18	72	1.08	22.85	6.72	6.31	16.1	11.0
	10–20	18	66	1.30	28.22	6.68	6.17	8.2	5.1
Pinyon/Juniper group	0–10	43	64	1.19	18.59	7.35	6.87	4.8	6.3
	10–20	33	58	1.35	25.43	7.56	7.01	3.3	2.0
Ponderosa pine	0–10	22	65	1.24	32.54	6.32	5.72	16.7	6.8
	10–20	19	57	1.54	38.94	6.49	5.81	11.0	3.0
Lodgepole pine	0–10	19	65	0.84	28.99	5.35	4.77	18.9	14.8
	10–20	19	57	1.30	35.75	5.54	4.85	22.5	9.5
Douglas fir	0–10	9	71	0.90	42.98	6.55	6.05	40.8	19.4
	10–20	5	66	1.21	50.04	6.45	5.77	31.3	10.2
Aspen	0–10	29	74	0.86	22.11	6.18	5.68	21.6	10.6
	10–20	26	70	1.10	26.10	6.18	5.62	17.3	9.3
Spruce/Fir group	0–10	29	72	0.69	25.93	5.76	5.22	16.8	15.3
	10–20	21	64	1.09	33.44	5.59	4.99	12.4	6.9
Western softwoods group	0–10	2	69	1.08	51.88	7.12	6.59	10.8	4.0
	10–20	2	65	1.28	56.31	6.65	6.18	9.2	4.9

[a]SQI = Soil Quality Index

Table E3b—Mean exchangeable cation concentrations in soil cores by forest type, Colorado, 2000-2004.

Forest type	Soil layer	Number of plots	1 M NH₄Cl Exchangeable cations Na	K	Mg	Ca	Al	ECEC
	cm				mg/kg			cmolc/kg
Deciduous oak woodland	0–10	18	10	280	306	3507	1	21.78
	10–20	18	19	231	299	3472	2	21.39
Pinyon/Juniper group	0–10	43	13	193	186	3599	1	20.58
	10–20	33	22	142	188	3646	2	20.64
Ponderosa pine	0–10	22	10	155	194	1816	2	11.22
	10–20	19	14	98	143	1367	1	8.39
Lodgepole pine	0–10	19	17	176	138	1174	57	8.44
	10–20	19	16	118	97	765	65	6.03
Douglas fir	0–10	9	11	263	249	2686	1	16.45
	10–20	5	13	233	273	2272	9	14.53
Aspen	0–10	29	8	350	259	2729	5	16.96
	10–20	26	13	269	184	1965	4	12.33
Spruce/Fir group	0–10	29	30	261	263	2475	62	17.49
	10–20	21	33	171	215	1546	78	12.97
Western softwoods group	0–10	2	21	401	186	2475	1	15.27
	10–20	2	14	427	212	2259	0	14.23

Table E3c—Mean extractable trace element concentrations in soil cores by forest type, Colorado, 2000-2004.

Forest type	Soil layer	Number of plots	1 M NH$_4$Cl Extractable							
			Mn	Fe	ni	Cu	Zn	Cd	Pb	S
	cm		- -*mg/kg*- -							
Deciduous oak woodland	0–10	18	6.4	0.04	0.07	0.00	0.03	0.10	0.03	770.0
	10–20	18	7.0	0.19	0.02	0.04	0.07	0.04	0.16	753.3
Pinyon/Juniper group	0–10	43	5.3	0.19	0.07	0.00	2.72	0.19	0.28	247.1
	10–20	33	3.5	0.01	0.02	0.07	0.09	0.04	0.20	285.5
Ponderosa pine	0–10	22	22.9	0.04	0.04	0.00	0.43	0.11	0.15	6.1
	10–20	19	9.6	0.10	0.02	0.05	0.19	0.06	0.14	5.8
Lodgepole pine	0–10	19	47.7	6.87	0.07	0.00	1.27	0.10	0.47	10.7
	10–20	19	9.1	5.52	0.03	0.03	1.34	0.06	0.49	7.2
Douglas fir	0–10	9	15.9	0.04	0.04	0.00	0.16	0.15	0.22	10.0
	10–20	5	5.0	0.02	0.05	0.02	0.03	0.03	0.23	5.5
Aspen	0–10	29	14.3	0.11	0.13	0.00	0.15	0.07	0.15	12.2
	10–20	26	10.2	0.39	0.01	0.00	0.16	0.03	0.14	12.5
Spruce/Fir group	0–10	29	35.6	3.72	0.06	0.00	0.84	0.13	0.42	15.0
	10–20	21	15.6	2.66	0.07	0.05	1.04	0.06	0.40	33.4
Western softwoods group	0–10	2	7.8	0.65	0.00	0.00	0.00	0.00	0.01	7.6
	10–20	2	6.0	0.00	0.00	0.00	0.00	0.01	0.09	22.8

Table E4—Total roundwood output by product, species group, and source of material, Colorado, 2002 (in thousand cubic feet).

Product and species group	Source of material			
	Growing-stock trees		Other sources	All sources
	Sawtimber	Poletimber		
Sawlogs				
Softwood	7,106	931	2,574	10,610
Hardwood	927	122	613	1,661
Total	8,033	1,053	3,186	12,272
Veneer logs				
Softwood	0	0	0	0
Hardwood	0	0	0	0
Total	0	0	0	0
Pulpwood				
Softwood	0	0	0	0
Hardwood	0	0	0	0
Total	0	0	0	0
Composite Panels				
Softwood	0	0	0	0
Hardwood	1,632	214	25	1,871
Total	1,632	214	25	1,871
Poles and posts				
Softwood	<0.5	302	96	399
Hardwood	<0.5	3	3	6
Total	<0.5	305	99	405
Other Miscellaneous				
Softwood	514	67	700	1,282
Hardwood	28	4	97	129
Total	542	71	797	1,410
Total Industrial Products				
Softwood	7,620	1,300	3,370	12,291
Hardwood	2,587	342	738	3,667
Total	10,207	1,642	4,108	15,958
Fuelwood				
Softwood	1	<0.5	15,053	15,054
Hardwood	<0.5	<0.5	3,928	3,928
Total	1	<0.5	18,981	18,983
All products				
Softwood	7,621	1,301	18,423	27,345
Hardwood	2,587	342	4,666	7,596
Total	10,208	1,643	23,090	34,941

USDA Forest Service Resour. Bull. RMRS-RB-11. 2010

105

Table E5—Volume of timber removals by source of material, species group, and removal type, Colorado, 2002 (in thousand cubic feet).

Removal type	Growing stock			Other sources			All sources		
	Softwoods	Hardwoods	Total	Softwoods	Hardwoods	Total	Softwoods	Hardwoods	Total
Roundwood products									
Saw logs	8,037	1,049	9,086	2,574	613	3,186	10,610	1,661	12,272
Veneer logs									
Pulpwood									
Composite products	0	1,846	1,846	0	25	25	0	1,871	1,871
Fuelwood	1	<0.5	1	15,053	3,928	18,981	15,054	3,928	18,983
Posts, poles, and pilings	302	3	305	96	3	99	399	6	405
Miscellaneous products	581	31	613	700	97	797	1,282	129	1,410
Total roundwood products	8,922	2,929	11,851	18,423	4,666	23,090	27,345	7,596	34,941
Logging residues	493	162	655	2,456	513	2,969	2,949	675	3,624
Total timber removals	9,414	3,091	12,505	20,880	5,179	26,059	30,294	8,270	38,564

USDA Forest Service Resour. Bull. RMRS-RB-11. 2010

Table E6—QA results for condition-level variables from 81 conditions in Colorado 2002 to 2006.

Variable	Tolerance	Percentage of data within tolerance				Number of times data exceeded tolerance				Records
		@1x	@2x	@3x	@4x	@1x	@2x	@3x	@4x	
Condition status	No tolerance	100.0%				0				81
Reserve status	No tolerance	97.5%				2				81
Owner group	No tolerance	98.8%				1				81
Forest type (Type)	No tolerance	89.3%				8				75
Forest type (Group)	No tolerance									
Stand size	No tolerance	86.7%				10				75
Regeneration status	No tolerance	100.0%				0				75
Tree density	No tolerance	100.0%				0				75
Condition nonsampled Reason	No tolerance	100.0%				0				1
Owner class	No tolerance	97.5%				2				81
Owner status	No tolerance	100.0%				0				2
Regeneration species	No tolerance									
Stand age	±10 %	96.0%	96.0%	96.0%	97.3%	3	3	3	2	75
Disturbance 1	No tolerance	86.7%				10				75
Disturbance year 1	±1 yr	40.0%	60.0%	60.0%	60.0%	3	2	2	2	5
Disturbance 2	No tolerance	75.0%				3				12
Disturbance year 2	±1 yr									
Disturbance 3	No tolerance	100.0%				0				3
Disturbance year 3	±1 yr									
Treatment 1	No tolerance	98.7%				1				75
Treatment year 1	±1 yr	100.0%				0				1
Treatment 2	No Tolerance	50.0%				1				2
Treatment year 2	±1 yr									
Treatment 3	No tolerance	100.0%				0				1
Treatment year 3	±1 yr									
Physiographic class	No tolerance	53.3%				35				75
Present nonforest use	No tolerance	100.0%				0				5
Regional variables										
Percent crown cover	±10 %	84.0%	94.7%	97.3%	98.7%	12	4	2	1	75
Percent bare ground	±10 %	86.7%	94.7%	94.7%	96.0%	10	4	4	3	75
Habitat type 1	No tolerance	37.3%				47				75
Habitat type 2	No tolerance	36.0%				48				75
Condition class number	No tolerance	98.8%				1				81

USDA Forest Service Resour. Bull. RMRS-RB-11. 2010

107

Table E7—QA results for tree variables from 2,266 Trees in Colorado 2002 to 2006.

Variable	Tolerance	Percentage of data within tolerance @1x	@2x	@3x	@4x	Number of times data exceeded tolerance @1x	@2x	@3x	@4x	Records
DBH	±0.1 /20 in.	90.1%	94.8%	96.3%	97.0%	179	94	66	54	1799
DRC	±0.1 /20 in.	54.2%	66.0%	73.9%	79.7%	214	159	122	95	467
Azimuth	±10 °	97.5%	99.0%	99.1%	99.2%	57	22	20	18	2266
Horizontal distance	±0.2 /1.0 ft	88.5%	94.2%	96.6%	97.7%	261	131	77	53	2266
Species	No tolerance	96.9%				71				2266
Tree genus										
Tree status	No tolerance	99.0%				22				2266
Rotten/Missing cull	±10 %	93.4%	97.3%	98.5%	99.0%	137	55	32	21	2065
Total length	±10 %	74.1%	91.8%	97.0%	98.8%	539	171	63	25	2080
Actual length	±10 %	65.9%	89.0%	96.3%	98.8%	28	9	3	1	82
Compacted crown ratio	±10 %	63.8%	88.9%	97.0%	99.0%	697	213	57	20	1923
Uncompacted crown ratio (P3)	±10 %	93.9%	98.6%	99.2%	99.8%	107	25	14	4	1764
Crown class	No tolerance	75.8%				465				1923
Decay class	±1 class	94.9%	99.7%	100.0%		16	1	0		314
Cause of death	No tolerance	57.1%				33				77
Mortality year	±1 yr	90.9%	100.0%			7	0			77
Condition class	No tolerance	98.9%				24				2266
New tree	No tolerance	93.5%				2				31
Regional variables										
Mistletoe	±1 class	97.5%	99.0%	99.8%	99.9%	49	19	4	2	1923
Number of stems	No tolerance	80.1%				93				467
Percent missing top	±10 %	97.9%	98.5%	99.0%	99.2%	44	30	20	16	2065
Sound dead	±10 %	85.9%	91.9%	94.6%	96.2%	291	168	111	79	2065
Form defect	±10 %	69.4%	84.1%	90.9%	93.6%	413	215	123	87	1350
Current tree class	No tolerance	95.4%				104				2251
Radial growth	±1 /20 inch	48.5%	69.8%	82.3%	91.1%	230	135	79	40	447
Breast height tree age	±10 %	41.7%	69.4%	84.7%	93.2%	179	94	47	21	307
Total tree age	±10 %	28.3%	48.9%	58.7%	70.7%	66	47	38	27	92
DRC using IW MQO	±0.2 in/stem	75.8%	87.4%	92.1%	94.4%	113	59	37	26	467
Horiz Dist-timberland	±0.2 /1.0 ft	96.7%	98.8%	99.1%	99.3%	60	21	16	12	1799
Horiz Dist-woodland	±0.2 /1.0 ft	57.0%	76.4%	86.9%	91.2%	201	110	61	41	467
Total Length: Saplings	±10 %	73.1%	92.5%	98.4%	100.0%	50	14	3	0	186
Actual Length: Saplings	±10 %	100.0%				0				1